School Law in Action:
101 Key Decisions with Guidelines
for School Administrators

School Law in Action:

101 Key Decisions with Guidelines for School Administrators

M. Chester Nolte

Professor of Educational Administration
University of Denver

Parker Publishing Company, Inc.   *West Nyack, N. Y.*

Second Printing.....March, 1972

PRINTED IN THE UNITED STATES OF AMERICA
ISBN—0-13-793703-2
B&P

To Harriet Ann

*Brevity is in writing
what charity is to all other virtues.*

—Sydney Smith, *Works*, i, 208 (1811)

The Value of This Book

The advantage of a case "brief" is that it condenses the salient points of a particular case and makes available in abbreviated form the issues and reasoning which the court used in arriving at its decision. Since many of the briefs you will find in this book are "landmark" cases having important effects on later case law, it is possible within the scope of 101 cases to present a wide range of developed principles of law upon which our country's educational enterprise currently rests.

Part One contains twenty-two briefs, mostly from the United States Supreme Court, which give a panoramic view of the whole range of educational litigation over the past 150 years. Landmark cases such as the Dartmouth College and Oregon cases are among those included in this section.

Part Two contains fourteen cases on the subject of employee negotiations and related problems—the right to strike, to assemble, to collectively bargain, and similar current litigation issues. Certainly no more important problem faces the school administrator and his board of education than that of how to deal with organizations representing groups of employees bent on discussing wages, hours, and conditions of employment. This section will be especially useful, therefore, to the busy school administrator who wishes to follow the reasoning behind some of the cases which have reached appellate courts in this country on the subject of collective bargaining in education.

Part Three deals with another fourteen cases, these on problems occasioned by student unrest, confrontations, dismissal and the disciplining of students in today's changing schools. Cases in which long hair, beards, student rights, and picketing have been litigated make up this section of the book.

Part Four is concerned with the tort liability of the school officials and staff—whether the teacher, administrator or school board member may be held liable in damages for injuries sustained by students or third parties on school property. This is a fast growing area of the law, and one which merits closer reading by most administrators. The manner in which the briefs are presented in this book enables the busy administrator to "get at" the reasoning of the courts in handing down their decisions.

Part Five covers another important area of the law, that of school board powers and duties. In an age when the powers of local boards of education seem to be waning, this section will prove especially helpful to those school board members who conscientiously wish to keep abreast of their responsibilities as members of the decision-making team in education.

Finally, Part Six deals with those two vitally important legal issues: racial discrimination and religious freedom. These seventeen cases bring together in one section the major briefs illustrating the principles of law which govern these two great movements as they are being fought in the nation's schools. Thus, the section rounds out the 101 cases which provide a quick and easy access to the inner workings of the common law as it affects the practice of school administration in the 1970's.

No book or set of books can make a school administrator into a lawyer, and this volume is not intended for that purpose. It is, however, the administrator's responsibility "to know the law" particularly as it affects him in his daily work. With this thought in mind, the present volume was written.

M. CHESTER NOLTE

Table of Contents

Part One: continued

PART TWO: Employee Negotiations and Related Problems   **69**

Part Two: continued

PART THREE: *Cases Related to Student Unrest,
Dismissal, and Discipline*   **101**

PART FOUR: *Tort Liability of the School Officials
and Staff*   **135**

Part Four: continued

PART FIVE: School Board Powers and Duties   **168**

**PART SIX: Racial Discrimination, Religious Freedom,
        and Dismissal Cases**   **201**

Part Six: continued

Table of Cases

Cases briefed in this volume are in italics. Cited cases
are in roman. References are to Case Number and to
Page.

PART ONE

Landmark Cases at Law
Which Shaped
the American School System

Part One

Landmark Cases at Law
Which Shaped the American
School System

*T*he casual reader could easily underestimate the importance of the courts upon our "American educational system," a system incidentally which, like Topsy, "just grew" because it had no model or plan by which it was to rise. Its brick and mortar were the pragmatic compromises of the time, its direction determined by the adolescence or relative maturity of the people's concepts of the issues and the place of their educational system in them at the moment. While such growth and direction may seem hit-or-miss, some of the decisions were clearly discernible and quite predictable from clues of other "landmark" cases, many of the clues hidden in dissenting opinions, to emerge when their time had come.

The purpose of Part One is to present an overview of these major cases which have shaped and will continue to shape the system of education unique to this country and to our time. The twenty-two selected cases are in brief form, with accompanying notes related to the work of the school administrator, school board member, or school attorney. The resulting array is, in effect, a legal history of the schools from the early Nineteenth Century to the present.

The cases range in time over a century and a half, from the *Dartmouth College* case in 1819 to the *Tinker* armband case settled by the United States Supreme Court in 1969. Their content is equally broad—from a decision that for school purposes a Chinese child is "colored," to a ruling that university students have a right to due process of law before dismissal for their participation in an off-campus sit-in demonstration. Hopefully, the cases reveal directional "straws in the wind" as they relate to four major concerns which have occupied the attention of the courts over the years.

In general, the courts have been called upon to settle, or to help the people settle, these issues: 1) the question of what kind or kinds of schools we should have, and the scope and nature of their work; 2) the question of the relationship of the schools operated by the state to organized religion; 3) the question of how each child, regardless of his race, creed, or country of origin, might achieve the American dream of equal educational opportunity; and, more recently, 4) the extent to which the citizen, teacher, scholar, or third party intervenor might enjoy guaranteed constitutional rights while in contact with the established educational system. That these issues are not yet settled is no indictment of the work of the courts; it is entirely possible that they will never be completely at rest.

The questions were prompted by man's eternal attempts to be free—religiously, politically, and economically—and grew naturally out of the fact that this country was founded on actions based upon this desire. Hindered by no pre-limiting constraints, and guided by the body of English law, the American pioneer expected something from his schools which no other country had been able to furnish—the educational savvy which would permit such freedoms to emerge. As a result, the major revolutions of our period of history, from the Reformation, through the American and French revolutions, the Industrial Revolution, the Revolution of Automation, and including the Revolution of Rising Expectations, have all found their way into the schools and are still in progress. Out of Luther's desire for greater religious freedom, for example, has emerged our preoccupation with the relationship between church and state. From our interest in political freedom, characterized by the work of Jefferson and Locke, has come the concept that man should be politically free.

While the Industrial Revolution affected the schools only obliquely, the technological impact of the Revolution of Automation has had quite a different effect. Coupled with the Revolution of Rising Expectations, the technological impact has Americans asking whether their schools are relevant to today's real world and whether the schools are equal to the task before them.

Most of the cases, but by no means all of them, are decisions handed down by what its critics call "The Black-Robed School Board," the United States Supreme Court. The cases in this first section, based as they are on fundamental issues, constitute a compendium of the "issues" over the years, and make for the careful reader a set of fascinating insights into how education evolved in this country. The reader will note a theme emerging through it all—the desire of Americans to provide schools which help them and their children to "secure the blessings of liberty" in our place and time. That this is an attainable goal appears not to be open to question.

1   *State Authority over Private Colleges*

The legislature of New Hampshire in 1816 passed an "act to amend the charter, and enlarge and improve the corporation of Dartmouth College," which brought the institution under public control because the new board of overseers was composed principally of public appointees and government officials. The original trustees refused to accept the amended charter and brought suit to recover the corporate property. The original charter had been granted by George III in 1769, conveying "forever" the right to govern the institution and fill vacancies in their own membership. The New Hampshire Superior Court upheld the legislative act of 1816 chiefly on the ground that the college was essentially a public corporation whose powers and franchises were exercised for public purposes and therefore subject to public control.

Relief Sought: An action of trover, to restore to the Trustees of Dartmouth College the book of records, the corporate seal, and other items then in the possession of the state.

Issue: May a state change a charter of a private institution (Dartmouth College) and, in effect, bring it under public control?

Holding of the Trial Court: In favor of the State of New Hampshire.

Holding of the Appellate Court: Judgment of the trial court reversed and annulled. Defendants to be assessed damages of $20,000 with costs of suit—4 Sup. Ct. (Wheat) 463.

Reasoning

The charter granted by the English Crown to the trustees in 1769 is a contract within the meaning of the Constitution. The charter was not dissolved by the Revolution. The act of the state legislature of New Hampshire altering the charter without the consent of the corporation is an act impairing the obligation of a contract, and is clearly in conflict with Art. I, sec. 10 of the United States Constitution. The action is therefore null and void. A state may alter such a contract or charter only when it reserves the right in the granting of the contract or charter. That a corporation is established for purposes of general charity, or for education generally, does not, *per se,* make it a public corporation, liable to the control of the legislature. The will of the state is substituted for the will of the donors in every essential operation of the college. . . . This may be for the advantage of this college in particular, and may be for the advantage of literature in general; but it is not according to the will of the donors, and is subversive of that contract on the faith of which their property was given. . . . The judgment of the state court must, therefore, be reversed.

Significance

A state's authority over private educational institutions is not unlimited. The Dartmouth College case opened the door to a system of private colleges and universities paralleling the state-supported higher educational institutions. This dual system has become one of the major strengths of American higher education through the intervening century and a half.

CASE CITATION: *Trustees of Dartmouth College v. Woodward, 17 U.S. (4 Wheat) 518 (N. H. 1819)*

2   State Authority over Private Education

In 1922, the Oregon legislature enacted a Compulsory Education Act which required every parent to send his child between 8 and 16 years of age to a public school. The Society of Sisters was an Oregon corporation "with power to care for orphans, educate and instruct the youth. . . ." The Hill Military Academy was likewise engaged in private education of boys between 5 and 21 years. The effect of the law would have been to close these schools. The statute was to go into effect in 1926, but before it could be brought, suit was filed in district court to restrain the state from enforcing the act.

Relief Sought: Reversal of decrees of the district court granting preliminary injunctions restraining the Governor of the State of Oregon from attempting to enforce an amendment to the school law requiring parents to send young children to the public schools of the state only.

Issue: Does the state have the power to require that its children must attend public schools only, rather than schools of parental choice?

Holding of the Trial Court: In favor of the plaintiffs, Society of Sisters and Hill Military Academy

Holding of the U.S. Supreme Court: Affirmed

Reasoning

Enforcing the act would result in real and irreparable injury to the plaintiffs, and would constitute an educational monopoly by the state. The child of a man is his, not the state's. . . . The child is not the mere creature of the state; those who nurture him and direct his destiny have the right, coupled with the high duty, to recognize and prepare him for additional obligations. Parents may direct the education of their children by choosing both teachers and places. Corporations cannot claim for themselves the liberty guaranteed by the Fourteenth Amendment, but they can claim protection under it for their business. The injunctions sought are not against the exercise of any proper power. The plaintiffs are asking protection against arbitrary, unreasonable, and unlawful interference with their patrons and the consequent destruction of their property and business, without due process of law. Rights granted by the United States Constitution may not be abridged by legislation which has no reasonable relation to some purpose within the competency of the state. The fundamental theory of liberty, upon which all governments in this union repose, excludes a general power of the state to standardize its children by forcing them to accept instruction from public schools only.

Significance

The court ruled that states may regulate schools, but the state may not force children to attend public schools only so long as private schools meet minimal standards established by the state. This case did for private elementary and secondary schools what the Dartmouth College case had done earlier for private higher educational institutions. Thus, elementary and secondary education, as well as higher education, is composed of a dual system of parallel institutions, one public and the other private in nature.

CASE CITATION: *Pierce, Governor of Oregon et al. v. Society of Sisters; Pierce, Governor of Oregon et al. v. Hill Military Academy, 268 U.S. 510, 45 Sup. Ct. 571, 69 L.Ed. 1070 (Oregon 1925)*

3   State Authority to Tax for a High School and to Employ a Superintendent

Plaintiff Stuart, a taxpayer, and two other taxpayers questioned the right of the school districts within the state to levy taxes for a high school, although they had no objection to such levy for common school purposes, and further objected that the specific district in question had no power to levy such a tax because no specific law had been passed permitting them to do so, nor did they have the right to employ a superintendent of schools.

Relief Sought: A restraining order barring the school district from collecting such portion of the school taxes earmarked for the support of a high school in the Village of Kalamazoo and the payment of the salary of the superintendent of schools.

Issue: May local school authorities by implication levy taxes upon the general public for the support of a high school and to make such instruction free to the school age children, and to employ and pay the salary of a superintendent?

Holding of the Trial Court: For defendant board of education

Holding of the Appellate Court: Affirmed

Reasoning

After noting with approval that the state had provided not only for the common schools but also for a state university, the court pointed out that failure to provide for high school education would seem inconsistent indeed. To the argument that classical and foreign languages were the accomplishment of the few, and not designed for the many, the court expressed surprise that anyone should question the right of the state to bring a liberal education within the grasp of the youth of all classes living within the state. Also since thirteen years of operation of a high school had preceded this action, the district was justified in making the levy.

The court further stated, using the above reasoning, that the district was within its powers to appoint a superintendent of schools and to pay him a salary to direct the work of the schools.

Significance

This case established the implied, as distinguished from the enumerated, right of the state to permit local school boards to establish high schools and to employ a superintendent of schools. The decision had an immediate effect on high school enrollments. Between 1870 and 1890, the number of high schools in the United States increased fivefold. Beginning in 1890, high school enrollments doubled each decade until 1920. The Kalamazoo decision, while not entirely responsible, nevertheless had a profound effect on the proliferation of secondary schools in this country during the latter years of the nineteenth century.

No longer was a common school education sufficient for America's children; a high school education became in effect the birthright of every child through his state's power to tax its inhabitants to insure this guarantee, set forth in the Kalamazoo case. This decision thus stands as a landmark on the educational horizon.

CASE CITATION: *Stuart et al. v. School District No. 1 of the Village of Kalamazoo, 30 Mich. 69 (1874)*

4   State Authority over the Curriculum

In 1919, shortly after World War I, the state legislature passed an act forbidding, under penalty of law, the teaching to a pupil of any language except English until the eighth grade had been successfully passed. Plaintiff Meyer, a teacher at Zion Parochial School, unlawfully taught reading of German to Raymond Parpart, ten years of age, who had not passed the eighth grade at the time. Plaintiff was convicted, and here sought reversal of his conviction (fine of $25 to $100 and 30 days in jail), on the grounds that the law deprived him of his liberty guaranteed under the Fourteenth Amendment.

Relief Sought: Declaration of error to a judgment of the Supreme Court of Nebraska affirming a conviction for infraction of a statute against teaching a foreign language to young children in school.

Issue: Does a state law forbidding the teaching of any modern foreign language to a child who has not yet passed the eighth grade invade the liberty guaranteed by the Fourteenth Amendment and exceed the power of the state?

Holding of the Trial Court: Conviction of the instructor Meyer

Holding of the Supreme Court of Nebraska: Judgment affirmed

Holding of the United States Supreme Court: Judgment reversed and case remanded for further proceedings

Reasoning

Imparting knowledge in a foreign language is not inherently immoral or inimical to the public welfare, and not a fit subject for prohibitory legislation. No evidence has ever been shown that it is harmful to learn a foreign language. The statute in question is not a legitimate exercise of the state's police power. The exercise of the police power can be justified only when it adds, in a substantial way, to the security of the fundamental rights of its citizens. The plaintiff taught this language in school as part of his occupation. Mere knowledge of the German language cannot reasonably be regarded as harmful. His right thus to teach and the right of parents to engage him so to instruct their children are within the liberty of the Fourteenth Amendment which states, "No State shall make or enforce any law which shall abridge the privileges or immunities of citizens of the United States; nor shall any state deprive any person of life, liberty, or property without due process of law. . . ."

Significance

Although education is primarily a function of the state, this right is subject to constitutional limitations. No state may enact a statute which interferes with an individual's constitutional right to engage in the practice of his legitimate profession or calling without first providing him due process of law. Parental rights to choose what type of education their children shall receive were further strengthened by the case. The federal Constitution being silent on the subject of education, education is thought to be a state function, but this authority is not unlimited when it comes into conflict with an individual's constitutionally guaranteed rights, as in this case. Statutes which are arbitrary and without reasonable relation to any end within the competency of the state must fall before the rights of the individual to practice his legitimate profession.

CASE CITATION: *Meyer v. Nebraska, 262 U.S. 390 (Nebraska 1923)*

5   State Authority to Establish Separate Schools for Negro Children

Plaintiff being a five-year-old colored child and a resident of Boston applied in April, 1847 to a member of the District Primary School Committee having under his charge the primary school nearest plaintiff's place of residence for admission to that school. Admission was denied on the ground of her being a colored person and of special provisions having been set up for special schools for colored students.

On February 15, 1848, the plaintiff went to the primary school nearest her residence and was on that day ejected from the school by the teacher. Prior to her ejection, she had made subsequent petitions to the general primary school committee which redirected plaintiff to the committee of the district giving the committee full power. Again application was denied plaintiff on account of her color. She then went to her closest school and was ejected.

Defendant school board claimed that at all times the student was welcome to attend the designated school for colored children. This school was in fact in the same immediate area as that school to which the plaintiff attempted to be admitted, but was rejected.

Relief Sought: Writ to compel the payment of damages by defendants under the statute which provides that any qualified child unlawfully excluded from public school instruction in this commonwealth shall recover damages against the city or town by which such public instruction is supported.

Issue: Does a ruling of the general school committee, in making provision for the instruction of colored children in separate schools established exclusively for them and prohibiting them from attending other public schools within the district, violate the provision that any child may not unlawfully be excluded from public school instruction in this commonwealth?

Holding of the Trial Court: In favor of defendant; plaintiff nonsuited.

Holding of the Appellate Court: Affirmed; plaintiff nonsuited.

Reasoning

Plaintiff was not unlawfully excluded from the public school nor was instruction closed to her. The defendant, by providing separate primary schools, had in effect complied with the statute requiring public school instruction to any child. Plaintiff, by her father not taking proper measure to obtain admission in the school provided, did in effect cause his child to be denied enrollment in the public schools.

Significance

The *Roberts* case was cited in a later case (see Case No. 6 *infra*) in Louisiana which set the pattern for separate but equal facilities for white and colored passengers in railroad coaches. Between 1849 and 1954 it was held in the common law that the general school committee had the right under the constitution to make provision for the instruction of colored children in separate schools established exclusively for them and to prohibit their attendance in other public schools in the same district. This concept of local board authority was overthrown in the *Brown* decision in 1954 in which the Supreme Court held that separate but equal facilities for the children of the races are inherently unequal, and therefore unconstitutional.

CASE CITATION: *Sarah C. Roberts v. The City of Boston, 59 Mass. (5 Cushing) 198 (1849)*

6 State Authority to Establish Separate Accommodations for White and Colored Passengers in Intra-State Railroad Travel

Petitioner, Homer A. Plessy, was a citizen of the United States, and a resident of the State of Louisiana, of mixed descent in the proportion of 7/8ths Caucasian and 1/8th Negro blood. The mixture was not discernible in him, and he often passed for white. On June 7, 1892, he engaged and paid for first class passage on the East La. Railway from New Orleans to Covington, entered the train and took a vacant seat in the passenger coach where white passengers were accommodated. The railroad company was a La. corporation and a common carrier subject to the applicable state laws. Petitioner was requested by the conductor under penalty of ejection and imprisonment under the law to vacate the seat and occupy a seat where passengers other than white were accommodated.

He refused to comply and was forcibly ejected and imprisoned in the parish jail. He sought relief in the courts.

Relief Sought: Error to the Supreme Court of Louisiana to review judgment of that court, denying petition of Homer A. Plessy for writs of prohibition and certiorari against John H. Ferguson, Judge of the Criminal Court for the Parish of Orleans.

Issue: Is a law requiring the separation of white and colored races in public conveyances a reasonable exercise of the police power of the state?

Holding of the Trial Court: Judgment for respondent State of Louisiana

Holding of the United States Supreme Court: Affirmed

Reasoning

Plaintiff's rights under the Thirteenth Amendment were not violated by the law in question since the Amendment deals with the abolition of slavery; similarly, the plaintiff's rights under the Fourteenth Amendment were not violated since the La. law applies only to railroads on an intrastate basis, and the Supreme Court can therefore take no action (since the prohibitions are upon interstate commerce). The statute is reasonable in that it is in accord with usage and custom, and it promotes the peace and comfort of the people. No badge of inferiority is stamped on the Negro under this statute, for his right to political and civil equality is not questioned nor injured in any way under it. The Constitution does not guarantee or provide the Negro with social equality. Mr. Justice Harlan in dissent made the now-famous remark that "the Constitution is color-blind," but he was in the minority. The majority holding that separate but equal facilities neither abridges the privileges or immunities of the colored man, deprives him of his property without due process of law, nor denies him equal protection of the laws, held sway until overthrown by *Brown* in 1954.

Significance

From this case emerged the doctrine of separate but equal facilities for the races. The court cited the *Roberts* (1849) case with approval (see Case No. 5 *supra*) and had far-reaching effects upon public school attendance for over half a century following its release. Despite Justice Harlan's admonition that the Constitution was color-blind, and that "in respect of civil rights, all citizens are equal before the law," the separate but equal doctrine of *Plessy v. Ferguson* controlled the law for years.

CASE CITATION: *Plessy v. Ferguson, 163 U.S. 537, 16 Sup.Ct. 1138, 41 L.Ed. 256 (La. 1896)*

AUTHOR'S COMMENTARY

The impact of the *Plessy* decision would not have been so great had the Court confined its attention to segregated transportation facilities, which have a limited effect on small numbers of the populace over relatively short periods of time. The Court, however, chose to go beyond the facts of the case under consideration in reaching its decision. Drawing on the *Roberts* case, the doctrine of "separate but equal" was thus extended to school cases. From this decision came the concept, later to become a blanket statement, that so long as separate facilities of an equal nature are provided, state-imposed segregation of the races is within constitutional limits.

Perhaps the most unfortunate part of the *Plessy* decision was the total disregard of Negro rights where plaintiff Plessy claimed that separation into separate railway cars worked to a psychological disadvantage for black passengers. Said the Court, in rejecting Plessy's contention:

> We consider the underlying fallacy of the plaintiff's argument (that separate but equal facilities for black and white passengers was psychologically damaging to Negroes) to consist in the assumption that enforced separation of the two races stamps the colored race with a badge of inferiority. If this be so, it is not by reason of anything found in the Act, but solely because the colored race choose to put that construction upon it.

It was this particular point in the *Plessy* decision which was struck down in the *Brown* decision (see Case No. 8, *infra*) fifty-eight years later, when the Warren Court held that separate but equal facilities for black and white school children "are inherently unequal." In the intervening years, the separate but equal doctrine was obviously headed for a "show-down" because of its difficulty of application and its obvious inequalities of treatment of Negroes. Aided by the doctrine established in *Plessy,* many southern states moved in the direction of depriving Negroes of other constitutional rights not theretofore in question. As a result of it, almost all phases of the life of the southern Negro suffered. The Negro schools, which were obviously separate, were generally by no means equal to their counterparts, the white schools. In effect, two different (but unequal) systems of education existed in these states, nor were the inequalities susceptible of resolution in the courts of law. So difficult was the "separate but equal" doctrine to administer that in effect the courts became their administrators, settling questions which arose over the administration of the schools.

In *Cumming v. Board of Education* (175 U.S. 528, Ga., 1899) the Supreme Court was faced with a problem in which a Georgia county maintained a white high school, but had closed the black high school on the ground that it could not afford both. Asserting that the benefits and burdens of public taxation must fall equally upon all citizens, the Court nonetheless held that inasmuch as the closing of the Negro high school was "only temporary" and, because it was based on economic pressures, Negro students were not deprived of their constitutional rights by the closing. The Court then upheld a state court ruling to the effect that the high school board could not be compelled under the Fourteenth Amendment to withhold funds for the white high school until matching funds for the Negro high school were provided. Thus, the doctrine outlined in *Plessy* was upheld.

In *Berea College v. Kentucky* (211 U.S. 45, Ky. 1908) the Court was faced with the question of whether a state-chartered college could separate the races for instructional purposes. The college was chartered by the State of Kentucky and was granted the privilege of providing instruction for both white and black students. Kentucky law provided that no educational institution could teach both white and black students at the same time. The validity of the statute was in question. Avoiding reference to the *Plessy* decision, the Court proceeded via another route to uphold the Kentucky statute. The rationale was that the state has an absolute right to control the corporation (in this case, the college which it had chartered) under its statutes providing for the separation of the races for educational instruction. The Court did recognize that if the state attempted to prevent an individual, as distinguished from a corporation, from teaching Negro and white students sitting together, such a statute would be in conflict with the federal Constitution because it would deny to individuals "powers which they may rightfully exercise." Thus, the *Plessy* doctrine was upheld but weakened because of the doubt here raised that there was a double standard, one for corporations and another for individuals.

In *Buchanan v. Warley* (245 U.S. 60, 1917), the Court refused to carry the doctrine into the field of housing. In denying a zoning ordinance which would have segregated an entire city by race, the Court said:

> It is urged that this proposed segregation will promote the public peace by preventing race conflicts. Desirable as this is, and important as is the preservation of the public peace, this aim cannot be accomplished by laws or ordinances which deny rights created or protected by the federal Constitution.

In *Gong Lum v. Rice, infra,* the Supreme Court met its first challenge to actual segregation in the public schools. Plaintiffs in the case, who were of Chinese descent, conceded control of the schools by the doctrine, but asserted that their child had been wrongly placed in the colored school instead of the white school, and sought to have the error rectified in court.

The doubt which had been building over the fairness of the separate but equal doctrine expressed in *Plessy* found its way into the decision. Chief Justice Taft, writing the majority opinion, expressed it in his assertion that had it not been so often previously approved, the *Plessy* doctrine might call in this case "for a very full argument and consideration," and apologized to plaintiffs when ruling against them using the words "assuming the cases (such as *Plessy* and others cited) to be rightly decided. . . ."

The following brief outlines the issues before the Court as it dealt with the problem of whether a Chinese child is white or "colored" for purposes of public education. The inadequacy of the separate but equal doctrine was apparent as early as 1927.

7 *State Authority to Regulate Schools and School Children*

Martha Lum was a nine-year-old Chinese youngster who attempted to attend the Rosedale School, a school for white children. After attending classes for one-half day, she was notified that she could not remain in that particular school because she was of Chinese descent and not a member of the Caucasian race. School officials indicated that she could attend the Negro school or go to a private school, but she could not attend the Rosedale School. Her father brought suit to compel the board to admit her to the white school.

Relief Sought: Reversal of State Supreme Court decision overruling plaintiff's request for an injunction to bar school board from taking action assigning Chinese child to the colored school.

Issue: May a state for school attendance purposes classify a Chinese child born in and a citizen of the United States in the same group as children with Negroid blood?

Holding of the Trial Court: In favor of the defendant school board

Holding of the State Supreme Court: Affirmed

Holding of the United States Supreme Court: Affirmed

Reasoning

The Court took the position that "colored races," as used in the Constitution of Mississippi, included broadly all other races than the white race, and was not strictly limited to persons of Negro blood.

The question was whether a Chinese citizen of the United States was denied equal protection under the Fourteenth Amendment when he was classified for educational purposes among the Negro population. The Court cited *Plessy v. Ferguson* in upholding the validity of separate facilities for white and colored children. The question then was, is a Chinese child colored within the meaning of the law? Most of the cases cited above, said the Court, it is true, arose over the establishment of separate schools as between white and black pupils, but we cannot think that the question is any different or that any different result can be reached, assuming the cases above cited to be rightly decided, where the issue is as between white pupils and the pupils of the yellow races. The decision is within the discretion of the state in regulating its public schools and does not conflict with the Fourteenth Amendment. The judgment of the Supreme Court of Mississippi is affirmed.

Significance

The Supreme Court continued until 1954 to assert the right of the various states to separate school children on the basis of race alone. Here the finding was tenuous at best and showed the extent to which the court went in upholding the right of the states to foster segregation in public education. Thus, the "separate but equal" theory established in *Plessy* was perpetuated here.

CASE CITATION: *Gong Lum v. Rice, 275 U.S. 78 (Miss. 1927)*

AUTHOR'S COMMENTARY

Numerous cases coming before the Supreme Court between 1927 and 1954 contained clues that the separate but equal doctrine was doomed. Four specific cases illustrate the trend, all cases involving Negro admittance to white graduate schools. In *Missouri ex rel. Gaines v. Canada* (305 U.S. 337, 1938) the Court struck down for the first time a statute providing for segregation in education. Missouri provided a law school for whites and offered to pay the tuition for any Missouri Negro who wished to attend a law school in an adjoining state. The Court rejected the contention of defendants that this arrangement met the test outlined in *Plessy*. The decision hinted at the possibility that *Plessy* meant more than merely providing equal but separate facilities, although it was based on the concept that a state is not providing equal facilities when it must depend upon another state's higher education facilities for its citizens of the black race.

Sipuel v. Board of Regents (332 U.S. 631, 1948), *Sweatt v. Painter* (339 U.S. 629, 1950) and *McLaurin v. Oklahoma State Regents* (339 U.S. 637, 1950) were to the same effect. The holdings added up to the opinion expressed in *Gaines:* that in the matter of public education, the races were not on an equal footing. Stating that there is "a vast difference—a Constitutional difference—between restrictions imposed by the state, which prohibit the intellectual comingling of students, and the refusal of individuals to comingle where the state presents no such bar," the Court refused in each case to uphold statutes separating the races for educational purposes. Thus, the eventual overthrow of the *Plessy* doctrine was foreseeable, the question being not whether it would be discarded but how. In 1954, the Court reversed its earlier separate but equal doctrine, and, in the *Brown* decision, concluded that "in the field of public education, the doctrine of 'separate but equal' has no place."

8   State Authority to Segregate Children on the Basis of Race

In each of the four cases Negro children were denied admission to the public schools attended by white children under state laws requiring or permitting segregated schools on account of race. There were findings below that the Negro and white schools involved had been equalized or were being equalized with respect to buildings, curricula, qualifications and salaries of teachers, and other tangible factors.

Relief Sought: In each of the four cases, minors of the Negro race, through their legal representatives, seek the aid of the courts in obtaining admission to the public schools of their respective communities on a nonsegregated basis.

Issue: May racial segregation of school children be maintained if the facilities of the two systems are equal but separate?

Holding of the U. S. District Court: Relief denied, on grounds that, although segregation does have a detrimental effect on Negro children, relief is denied because Negro and white schools are substantially equal with respect to tangible factors involved.

Holding of the U. S. Supreme Court: Reversed

Reasoning

Education is perhaps the most important function of state and local governments. Compulsory school attendance laws and the great expenditures for education both demonstrate our recognition of the importance of education to our democratic society. . . . In these days, it is doubtful that any child may reasonably be expected to succeed in life if he is denied the opportunity of an education. Such an opportunity, where the state has undertaken to provide it, is a right which must be made available to all on equal terms. . . . Does segregation of children in public schools solely on the basis of race, even though the physical facilities and other "tangible" factors may be equal, deprive the children of minority groups of equal educational opportunities? We believe that it does. We conclude that in the field of public education the doctrine of "separate but equal" has no place. Separate educational facilities are inherently unequal. Therefore, we hold that the plaintiffs and others similarly situated for whom the actions have been brought are, by reason of the segregation complained of, deprived of the equal protection of the laws guaranteed by the Fourteenth Amendment.

Significance

Few cases in our history have triggered more discussion or litigation than this case, and its fine points are still being hammered out. In 1955, the Court ruled that all cases arising under the *Brown* decision should come under the jurisdiction of the federal district courts, bypassing the state court systems. These cases, too numerous to mention here, are recommended in those areas for further reading where problems may arise in school integration both North and South.

CASE CITATION: *Brown v. Board of Education of Topeka, 347 U.S. 483 (Kans. 1954)*

9   State Authority to Provide Free Textbooks to Parochial School Children

A state statute authorized the state to provide school textbooks free of charge to all children regardless of whether they attended a public or a non-public school. Plaintiff, a taxpayer and citizen of the State of Louisiana, claimed that the act violated the United States Constitution, in that it amounted in effect to the taking of private property for a private purpose without due process of law. If diversion of public funds is thus permitted, plaintiff claimed, under the same reasoning, the state may be prevented from taxing those who support only private schools.

Relief Sought: Taxpayer seeks restraining order to prevent the State Board of Education from purchasing school textbooks and supplying them free of cost to private and parochial school children.

Issue: May public tax moneys levied and collected by the state be used to purchase textbooks for children attending private and parochial schools?

Holding of the Trial Court: Injunction denied

Holding of the Court of Appeals: Judgment affirmed

Holding of the United States Supreme Court: Judgment affirmed

Reasoning

The schools are not the beneficiaries of this state gift, but the children. What the statute contemplates is that the same books that are furnished children attending public schools shall be furnished children attending private schools. It is only the use of the books that is granted to the children, or in other words, the books are lent to them. This action is not in violation of the Fourteenth Amendment which would constitute the taking of private property without due process of law. The schools are not the beneficiaries, the children are. The taxing power of the state is being exerted for a public purpose. Individual interests are aided only as the common interest (of the state) is safeguarded. The state legislature does not segregate private schools, or their pupils, as its beneficiaries, or attempt to interfere with any matters of exclusively private concern. Its interest is education, broadly; its method, comprehensive.

Significance

The so-called "child-benefit theory" established in this case was further expanded in the *Everson* case seventeen years later (see Case No. 10 *infra*). No doubt it had a profound influence on later developments such as the use of public moneys for private and parochial schools in the Elementary and Secondary Education Act (1965), and the New York School Textbook Statute (1967). The point made here, that the benefit from such a practice is to the child and the state, rather than to the individual school, is still being debated.

CASE CITATION: *Cochran v. Louisiana State Board of Education, 281 U.S. 370 (La. 1930)*

10 State Authority to Provide Free Transportation to Parochial School Children

Plaintiff, a taxpayer of the district, brought suit questioning the legality of a New Jersey statute authorizing boards of education to make rules and contracts for transportation of children to and from all schools except those private schools being operated for profit. Defendant school board had reimbursed parents for fare paid to public carriers for transportation of children to public and Catholic schools. Plaintiff argued that the statute authorized the use of tax money from private property to be bestowed upon others for private usage in violation of the due process clause of the Fourteenth Amendment. Also, the statute forces taxpayers, plaintiff claimed, to support schools dedicated to establishment of the Catholic faith in violation of the First Amendment. This violates the doctrine which says that Church and State shall be separate.

Relief Sought: Injunction to prevent a board of education from reimbursing parents of parochial school pupils for free transportation to and from their schools.

Issue: May a board of education, acting under statute, use public funds to pay for the transportation of pupils attending non-public schools?

Holding of the Trial Court: In favor of defendant school board

Holding of the Court of Errors and Appeals: Affirmed

Holding of the United States Supreme Court: Affirmed

Reasoning

Legislation intended to facilitate the opportunity of children to get a secular education serves a public purpose (citing *Cochran, supra*). The same thing is true of legislation to reimburse needy parents or all parents for payment of fares so they can ride on public buses rather than risk traffic hazards of walking or "hitchhiking." Subsidies and loans to individuals, such as farmers, home owners, and to privately-owned transportation systems, have been commonplace in state and national history. The First Amendment does not prohibit New Jersey using tax funds to pay bus fares of parochial or public school students. The Court has said that parents may send their children to a religious rather than a public school if the school meets secular educational requirements. The state contributes no money to the schools. It does not support them. It does no more than provide a way to get to and from school regardless of religion. The fact that a state law, passed to satisfy a public need, coincides with the personal desires of the individuals most directly affected is certainly an inadequate reason for us to say that a legislature has erroneously appraised the public need. The First Amendment has erected a wall between the church and the state; this wall must be kept high and impregnable. We could not approve the slightest breach. The State of New Jersey has not breached it here.

Significance

The "child benefit theory" is strengthened and upheld. Four justices dissented saying that to compel a man "to furnish contributions of money for the propagation of opinions which he disbelieves is sinful and tyrannical." The court in effect said that a state has the power to enact legislation to serve a public purpose, which includes getting pupils to and from accredited schools.

CASE CITATION: *Everson v. Board of Education, 330 U.S. 1 (N.J. 1947)*

11   State Authority to Use Public Schools for Religious Instruction; Released Time

The Champaign board agreed to religious instruction in the public schools under a "released time" arrangement. A taxpaying parent alleged that the permission granted was in violation of the First and Fourteenth Amendments. The public schools allowed teachers from various religious faiths to come into the school for the purpose of teaching religion one-half hour each week. The religious teachers kept records of attendance and turned them over to the regular teachers. Those students who did not wish to attend the religious class were placed in a separate room; the religious classes themselves were held in the regular classrooms of the school.

Relief Sought: Mandamus to compel defendant board of education to adopt rules and regulations prohibiting religious instruction in public schools of Champaign.

Issue: Does the board of education have the right to release pupils during school hours for the purpose of attending religious education classes held on the school premises?

Holding of the Trial Court: Mandamus denied

Holding of the United States Supreme Court: Reversed

Reasoning

Under the foregoing facts, the practice of religious instruction on public school property is unconstitutional. The operation of the state's compulsory education system thus assists and is integrated with the program of religious instruction carried on by separate religious sects. Pupils compelled by law to go to school for secular education are released in part from their legal duty upon the condition that they attend the religious classes. This is beyond all question a utilization of the tax-established and tax-supported public school system to aid religious groups to spread their faiths. And it falls squarely under the ban of the First Amendment (made applicable to the states by the Fourteenth Amendment). Neither the state nor the federal government can set up a church. Neither can pass laws which aid one religion, aid all religions, or prefer one religion over another. . . . In the words of Jefferson, the clause against establishment of religion by law was intended to erect "a wall of separation between Church and State." (quoting from *Everson*.) The First Amendment rests upon the premise that both religion and government can best work to achieve their lofty aims if each is left free from the other within its respective sphere. The First Amendment has erected a wall between Church and State which must be kept high and impregnable.

Significance

An arrangement to release school children from school hour requirements to attend religious instructional classes held in the public school classrooms as practiced in the Champaign plan is unconstitutional, and violative of the First Amendment "establishment" clause. Apparently, the prohibited part is not releasing children from their obligations under compulsory attendance laws, but to the use of school facilities for religious purposes, amounting, so said the Court, to an establishment of religion by a state.

CASE CITATION: *Illinois ex rel. McCollum v. Board of Education, 333 U.S. 203 (Ill. 1948)*

12   State's Authority to Release Children to Attend Religious Classes off School Property; Released Time

New York City had a program permitting public schools to release students during the school day so that they may leave the school buildings and school grounds and go to religious centers for religious instruction or devotional exercises. A student was released on written request of his parents. Those not released were to stay in the classrooms. The churches made weekly reports to the schools, sending a list of children who had been released from public schools but who had not reported for religious instruction.

Relief Sought: Court order to stop board of education from releasing public school pupils to engage in "released time" religious classes off
school property.

Issue: What is the constitutionality of a plan allowing religious instruction
on a "released time" basis in the New York City public schools?

Holding of the N.Y. Court of Appeals: The plan does not violate the constitution

Holding of the U.S. Supreme Court: Affirmed

Reasoning

This "released time" program involves neither religious instruction in public
school classrooms nor the expenditure of public funds. . . . We distinguish between this plan and the *McCollum* case. . . . There is no evidence of coercion
to get public school students into religious classrooms. If in fact coercion were
used, if it were established that any one or more teachers were using their office
to persuade or force students to take the religious instruction, a wholly different
case would be presented. Hence we put aside that claim of coercion both as
respects the "free exercise" of religion and the "establishment of religion" within
the meaning of the First Amendment. . . . We would have to press the concept
of separation of Church and State to (very grave) extremes to condemn the
present plan on constitutional grounds. . . . A Catholic student applies to his
teacher for permission to leave the school during hours on a Holy Day of Obligation to attend a mass. A Jewish student asks his teacher for permission to be
excused for Yom Kippur. A Protestant wants the afternoon off for a family bap-
tismal ceremony. In each case the teacher requires parental consent in writing. In
each case the teacher, in order to make sure the student is not a truant, goes
further and requires a report from the priest, rabbi, or the minister. The teacher
in other words cooperates in a religious program to the extent of making it possible for her students to participate in it. Whether she does it occasionally for a
few students, regularly for one, or pursuant to a systematized program designed to
further the religious needs of all the students does not alter the character of the
act. . . . Our individual preferences . . . are not the constitutional standard.
The constitutional standard is the separation of Church and State. The problem,
like many problems in constitutional law, is one of degree.

Significance

The Court was divided on this issue with Justices Black, Frankfurter, and
Jackson dissenting. The majority opinion suggests that being dismissed from
school to attend released time religious classes is on a par with being dismissed to
go to mass, Yom Kippur, or other religious rite. Anyway, the New York plan was

held legal while that in which public school buildings were used for religious purposes was struck down. This is the present status of the law on released time.

CASE CITATION: *Zorach v. Clauson, 343 U.S. 306 (N.Y. 1952)*

13   State Authority to Require the Flag Salute as a Condition of Attendance at a Public School

Lillian Gobitis, aged twelve, and her brother William, aged ten, were expelled from the Minersville (Pa.) schools for refusing to salute the flag as part of a daily exercise. The Gobitis family was affiliated with a group of Jehovah's Witnesses, who claimed that saluting the flag was equivalent to worshipping an image contrary to a fundamental of their faith, which was in line with the biblical admonition "Thou shalt not make unto thee any graven image of anything in heaven above or in the earth beneath; thou shalt not bow down to them nor serve them." The Gobitis children were within the compulsory school attendance age; hence, were being deprived of a free education by this action of the board.

Relief Sought: To enjoin school authorities from enforcing participation in the flag salute ceremonies as a condition of attendance at the public schools.

Issue: May a school board require that a public school student salute the flag as a condition of attendance in a public school?

Holding of the Trial Court: In favor of the Gobitis family

Holding of the U.S. Supreme Court: Reversed

Reasoning

Mr. Justice Frankfurter in writing the majority opinion said, "National unity is the basis of national security. The ultimate foundation of a free society is the binding tie of cohesive sentiment. The flag is a symbol of our national unity, transcending all internal differences, however large, within the framework of the Constitution. It is the symbol of the nation's power, the emblem of freedom in its truest, best sense. It signifies government resting on the consent of the governed, liberty regulated by law, and the protection of the weak against the strong. A society which is dedicated to the preservation of these ultimate values of civilization may in self-protection utilize the educational process for inculcating those almost unconscious feelings which bind men together in a comprehending loyalty, whatever may be their lesser differences and difficulties." We live by symbols and the flag is a symbol of our national unity. Some (symbols) may seem harsh and some foolish. However, the end is legitimate. We are dealing with an interest inferior to none in the hierarchy of legal values—our national unity, which is the basis of our national security.

Significance

National security in 1940 was more important to the court than the idea of individual liberties guaranteed in the First Amendment. A board may require the flag salute as a condition of public school attendance, said the Court (overruled in *Barnette,* see Case No. 14 *infra*) .

CASE CITATION: *Minersville School District v. Gobitis, 310 U.S. 586 (Pa. 1940)*

14   State Authority to Require the Flag Salute as a Condition of Attendance at a Public School

Following the Gobitis decision, the W. Va. State Board of Education adopted a resolution requiring "all teachers and pupils (to) participate in the salute honoring the Nation represented by the Flag; provided, however, that refusal to salute the Flag shall be regarded as an act of insubordination, and shall be dealt with accordingly." Those who refused to obey this resolution were expelled and could not be readmitted until they complied. Meanwhile, the student was considered "unlawfully absent" and could be proceeded against as a delinquent. His parents or guardians were liable to prosecution, and if convicted, were subject to fines not exceeding fifty dollars ($50.00) and a jail term not exceeding thirty days. Plaintiffs were Jehovah's Witnesses and called upon the Supreme Court to reconsider its earlier decision in Gobitis, *supra.*

Relief Sought: Cancellation of a school requirement that pupils must salute the flag and pledge allegiance to it.

Issue: Can a flag salute be imposed upon an individual student by official action of a state body or is such a requirement basis for expulsion?

Holding of the Trial Court: For plaintiffs

Holding of the United States Supreme Court: Affirmed

Reasoning

Mr. Justice Jackson delivered the opinion of the majority (8-1). There is no doubt that, in connection with the pledge, the flag salute is a form of utterance. Symbolism is a primitive but effective way of communicating ideas. It is not clear whether the regulation contemplates that pupils forego any contrary convictions of their own and become unwilling converts to the prescribed ceremony or whether it will be acceptable if they simulate assent by words without belief and by a gesture barren of meaning. Must a government of necessity be too strong for the liberties of its people, or too weak to maintain its own existence? The answer in the past has been in favor of strength. But the Fourteenth Amendment, as now applied to the states, protects the citizen against the State itself and all of its creatures, boards of education being no exception. That (boards) are educating the young for citizenship is reason for scrupulous protection of Constitutional freedoms of the individual, if we are not to strangle the free mind at its source and teach youth to discount important principles of our government as mere platitudes. Local authorities, in compelling the flag salute and pledge, transcend Constitutional limitations on their power and invade the sphere of intellect and spirit which it is the purpose of the First Amendment to our Constitution to reserve from all official control.

Significance

If there is a "clear and present danger" to the state, the state may then control and limit individual rights. But when, as here, there is no such condition or circumstance, individual liberty must transcend the right of the state to control the minds of its citizens, particularly if the citizens are children of tender years. The *Gobitis* decision was reversed, and its reversal stands today as the law of the land.

CASE CITATION: *West Virginia State Board of Education v. Barnette, 319 U.S. 624 (W. Va. 1943)*

15   State Authority to Require Recitation of a Prescribed Prayer in Public Schools

Plaintiff Engel's son was enrolled in the New Hyde Park district, which by resolution directed the recitation of the following prayer as a daily procedure after the salute to the flag: "Almighty God, we acknowledge our dependence upon Thee, and we beg Thy blessings upon us, our parents, our teachers, and our Country. Amen." Parents of various religious faiths, as well as one non-believer, with children attending the New Hyde Park schools, instituted court proceedings to discontinue use of the prayer on the ground that the prayer and the manner and setting in which it was said were contrary to their religious beliefs and practices. The board directed that no child should in any way be coerced to participate in the recital, and parents were allowed to request that their child should not participate, if they so desired.

Relief Sought: Writ to prohibit state board of regents from requiring a 22-word prayer in the public schools of New York.

Issue: May a state board of regents compose and require the recitation of a non-denominational prayer in public schools if student participation is not compulsory?

Holding of the Trial Court: For plaintiffs

Holding of the U.S. Supreme Court: Affirmed

Reasoning

Is the prescribed prayer a violation of the Establishment Clause of the First Amendment? We believe that it is. Religion has been closely identified with our history and government. We are a religious people whose institutions presuppose a Supreme Being. The history of man is inseparable from the history of religion. The state is firmly committed to a position of neutrality. It certainly may be said that the Bible is worthy of study for its literary and historical qualities. Nothing we say here indicates that such study of the Bible or of religion, when presented objectively as part of a secular program of education, may not be effected consistent with the First Amendment. The Establishment Clause of the First Amendment was intended to stand as a guarantee that "neither the power nor the prestige" of the government shall be used to support or influence the kinds of prayers the American people may make. The Fourteenth Amendment was added to strengthen this position with the individual states. The major consideration of both the First and Fourteenth Amendments was the historically proven fact that a union of government and religion tends to destroy government and to degrade religion.

Significance

Prior to 1962 the state courts had been dealing with separation of Church and State questions. This case raised the question whether a state-prescribed prayer, even one of a "non-denominational" nature, violates the Establishment Clause of the First Amendment, even though students may be excused on advice and consent of their parents from participation in the required recitation of the prayer.

CASE CITATION: *Engel v. Vitale, 370 U.S. 421 (N.Y. 1962)*

AUTHOR'S COMMENTARY

In *Everson v. Board of Education* (330 U.S. 1, N.J. 1947, Case No. 10, *supra*) the United States Supreme Court declared for the first time that the establishment clause, as well as the free exercise clause of the First Amendment, was applicable to the state through the due process clause of the Fourteenth Amendment. A similar child benefit argument had been previously upheld in the textbook case of *Cochran v. Board of Education* (281 U.S. 370, La. 1930, Case No. 9, *supra*). However, the basis for the Court's decisions in both cases was the federal Constitution, leaving unanswered whether similar fact situations in states other than New Jersey (*Everson*) and Louisiana (*Cochran*) violated state constitutional provisions. This was considered to be a matter for the various states to settle in their own state courts.

In 1952, the Court carved an exception to its interpretation of "establishment" in *Zorach v. Clauson* (343 U.S. 306, N.Y. 1952, Case No. 12, *supra*) by allowing "released time" for public school children to receive religious instruction on school time, although, unlike *McCollum,* not on school property. Support for the *Zorach* decision was in part based upon the parental rights argument, outlined first in *Pierce v. Society of Sisters* (268 U.S. 510, Ore. 1925, Case No. 2, *supra*) in which it was asserted that the parents might choose to educate their children in parochial schools instead of public schools. The reasoning was that inasmuch as parents may choose to meet all educational requirements via parochial schools, there was no violation of the First Amendment where the state releases a child for one hour a week to fulfill a similar religious purpose.

Little by little, the meaning of the "separation of Church and State" doctrine upon which this government was based came into focus as the Court continued to deal with school problems associated with the concept. In *Engel v. Vitale* (370 U.S. 421, N.Y. 1962, Case No. 15 *supra*) the Court further clarified its position on "establishment" in denying to the State of New York the power to require a state-composed prayer in the public schools' opening exercises. This was the first court test of the problem of prayers in public schools by the Supreme Court, since such matters had been uniformly left to the state courts theretofore.

The states in 1962 were by no means uniform on rules governing the recitation of prayers and the reading of the Bible in public schools. Twenty-six states, principally in the East and South, required or permitted Bible reading and often the Lord's Prayer, either by law or regulation of the state board of education. The District of Columbia and these eleven states *required* such observances in 1962: Alabama, Arkansas, Delaware, Florida, Georgia, Idaho, Maine, Massachusetts, New Jersey, Pennsylvania, and Tennessee.

In these fifteen states, Bible reading and/or prayers were *permitted* in 1962: Colorado, Hawaii, Indiana, Iowa, Kansas, Kentucky, Maryland,

Minnesota, Mississippi, New Hampshire, New York, North Dakota, Ohio Oklahoma, and Texas.

In these ten states, the offering of prayers and the reading of the Bible were *prohibited* in 1962: Alaska, Arizona, California, Illinois, Louisiana, Nebraska, Utah, Washington, Wisconsin, and Wyoming. In a survey of religious exercises commonly found in the public schools of the nation in that same year, a little more than half indicated they provided homeroom devotional services held in the school classrooms during school hours. The heaviest concentration of such practices was found in the East and South, with only scattered practice of this nature in the West and Southwest.

Thus, the framework against which the Supreme Court viewed the *Engel* question was far from clear or in focus. A wide divergency of practice and belief was evidenced throughout the country. The Supreme Court evidently was influenced by the divergency which it found in making its decision that the government must be "neutral" in matters affecting separation of Church and State.

16   State's Authority to Require Bible Reading and/or the Recitation of Prayers in the Public Schools

Pennsylvania law required that "At least ten verses from the Holy Bible shall be read, without comment, at the opening of each public school on each school day. Any child shall be excused from such Bible reading, upon the written request of his parent or guardian." The Board of School Commissioners of Baltimore City Schools adopted a resolution providing for the holding of opening exercises in the schools of the city, consisting primarily of the reading, without comment, of a chapter of the Holy Bible and/or the use of the Lord's Prayer. In both instances, plaintiffs attacked the rule as threatening their religious liberties, and amounting in effect to an establishment of religion by the state and its subdivisions.

Relief Sought: Relief from a Pennsylvania statute and a Baltimore school board regulation requiring that schools begin each day with readings from the Bible.

Issue: Do the practices complained of and the laws requiring them amount to an unconstitutional overreach in the state's powers and to an establishment of religion?

Holding of the Courts below: For the Schempp's, upheld; for Mrs. Murray, rejected

Holding of the United States Supreme Court: For the plaintiffs in each case

Reasoning

It is true that religion has been closely identified with our history and government. We have asserted this relationship in other cases (citing cases). Sixty-four percent of our people have church membership, while less than three percent profess no religion whatever. Our national life therefore reflects a religious people. The government is neutral, and, while protecting all, it prefers none, and it disparages none. There cannot be the slightest doubt that the First Amendment reflects the philosophy that Church and State should be separated. The separation must be complete and unequivocal. The practices complained of were prescribed as part of the curricular activities of students who are required by law to attend school. They were held in the school buildings under the supervision and with the participation of teachers employed in those schools, which is in direct violation of the rights of the plaintiffs. We have come to recognize through bitter experience that it is not within the power of government to invade that citadel (of the individual heart and mind), whether its purpose or effect be to aid or oppose, to advance or retard. In the relationship between man and religion, the state is firmly committed to a position of neutrality.

Significance

The Schempp decision continued in the tradition of *Everson* and *Engel*. Criticisms were numerous that the Court was establishing a "rule of the minority" since it tended to favor those who objected to any mention of God in the public schools. The schools were characterized as "Godless" and "irreligious" by some, but in the main there was an awareness that the decision was basically necessary in a pluralistic society.

CASE CITATION: *School District of Abington Township v. Schempp, and Murray v. Curlett, 374 U.S. 203 (Pa. and Md., 1963)*

AUTHOR'S COMMENTARY

Whereas the *Schempp and Murray* cases were decided on the basis of the Establishment Clause of the First Amendment as applied to the states through the Fourteenth Amendment, a similar case bottomed on the Free Exercise Clause was handed down by the Supreme Court at the same time. In *Sherbert v. Verner*, 31 L.W. 4719, S.C. 1963, the Court dealt with the question of whether a South Carolina statute abridged plaintiff's right to the free exercise of her religious belief secured under the First Amendment.

The decision was to the effect that it did infringe upon her rights and was therefore unconstitutional.

Appellant, a member of the Seventh Day Adventist Church, was discharged by a South Carolina employer because she would not work on Saturday, the Sabbath day in her faith. She had worked in the mills for some time on a five-day week, but the mill where she was employed went to a six-day week, and she was discharged. When she was unable to obtain employment other than that to which she had been giving her attention, and because of her religious scruples she would not take Saturday work, she filed a claim for unemployment compensation benefits under the South Carolina Unemployment Compensation Act. That statute provided that to be eligible for benefits, a claimant "must be able to work and available for work," and further that a claimant is ineligible for benefits "if he has failed, without good cause, to accept available suitable work when offered him by the employer."

When she was refused benefits under the law, she sought to have the decision of the Employment Security Commission overthrown by the court of common pleas of her county, but she lost the case in the South Carolina Supreme Court. Maintaining that a constitutional issue was involved, she appealed to the United States Supreme Court. The Court held the statute unconstitutional.

The reasoning of the Court is interesting. "Here," the Court said, "not only is it apparent that appellant's declared ineligibility for benefits derives solely from the practice of her religion, but the pressure upon her to forego that practice is unmistakable. The ruling forces her to choose between following the precepts of her religion and forfeiting benefits, on the one hand, and abandoning one of the precepts of her religion in order to accept work, on the other hand. Governmental imposition of such a choice puts the same kind of burden upon the free exercise of religion as would a fine imposed against appellant for her Saturday worship.

"In holding as we do, plainly we are not fostering the 'establishment' of the Seventh Day Adventist religion in South Carolina, for the extension of unemployment benefits to Sabbatarians in common with Sunday worshippers reflects nothing more than the governmental obligation of neutrality in the face of religious differences, and does not represent that involvement of religious with secular institutions which it is the object of the Establishment Clause to forestall. Nor do we, by our decision today, declare the existence of a constitutional right to unemployment benefits on the part of all persons whose religious convictions are the cause of their unemployment. This is not a case in which an employee's religious convictions serve to make him a nonproductive member of society."

Although this is not a school case, it has implications for the school administrator since it tends to clarify the meaning of the free exercise clause of the First Amendment. Both *Schempp* and *Sherbert* proclaim the government's neutrality in matters of religion.

Under the First Amendment, the Court said, the government is obliged to protect religious rights without fostering a state religion; the free exercise of religion clause must be respected, even as the establishment of a state religion is to be avoided.

Considered together, *Schempp* and *Sherbert* reflect an impression of a Court which is not anti-religious at all, but much more in sympathy with the problems of a pluralistic society, while at the same time preserving a proud national religious heritage, than many of its critics would give it credit for.

Reactions to the *Schempp* decision were varied. In *Sills v. Board of Education*, 200 A.2d 817, N.J. 1963 a superior court was faced with interpreting a New Jersey statute "almost identical" with that involved in *Schempp*, which required the reading without comment in each public school classroom of at least five verses from the Old Testament. Another act outlawed all religious services in the public schools except Bible reading and recitation of the Lord's Prayer. A local board of education declared that the Supreme Court decisions were not directly applicable to the New Jersey statutes. But the court pointed out that one does not have to be a party to a case to be bound thereby. Furthermore, the statute, if allowed to stand, could cause the teachers to violate their oath of allegiance to uphold the United States Constitution and could subject them to federal criminal prosecution. The acts complained of were therefore unconstitutional.

Similarly, in *Attorney General v. School Committee*, 199 N.E.2d 553, Mass. 1964, and *Johns v. Allen*, 231 F.Supp. 852, Md. 1964, the courts rejected pleas for continuation of Bible reading and the holding of religious exercises. In *Adams v. Engelking*, 232 F.Supp. 666, Idaho 1964, a federal district court rejected the idea that a state may enact a statute requiring daily reading of the Bible in all public schools of the state. Such a measure, said the Court, is plainly in violation of the Establishment of Religion Clause of the First Amendment, a question "which was settled in *Schempp*."

In *Chamberlin v. Dade County Board of Public Instruction*, 84 S.Ct. 1272, 1964, injunctions were sought to halt regular Bible reading in public school assemblies, recitation of the Lord's Prayer, conduct of baccalaureate programs, a religious census among children, and a religious test for teachers (teachers were asked, "Do you believe in God?"). The Florida Supreme Court refused to halt the practices, but the United States Supreme Court vacated the judgment, and remanded the case for consideration in the light of the *Schempp* decision. The Florida court defied the Supreme Court's decision, and declared that the statute relating to Bible reading was intended merely as a secular means of inculcating good moral behavior in children. Upon appeal, the U.S. Supreme Court held that part of the statute relating to Bible reading should be rejected, but dismissed the other questions "for want of properly presented federal questions." Thus, the question of baccalaureate exercises of a religious nature, a religious census among students, and the religious test for teachers went unsettled, although there seemed to be a tendency of the High Court to feel that a religious test required of teachers might well "raise a substantial question of constitutionality."

17   *State's Right to Provide Free Textbooks to Pupils Enrolled in Parochial and Private Schools*

New York law required local public school authorities to lend textbooks free of charge to all students in grades 7 through 12, students attending private schools included.

Relief Sought: Action to determine the validity of a New York statute requiring school districts to purchase and loan textbooks to students enrolled in parochial as well as in public and private schools.

Issue: Does the statute in question amount to an establishment of religion?

Holding of the Lower Courts: The New York Supreme Court, Albany County, held the law unconstitutional; the appellate court reversed this ruling. The New York Court of Appeals affirmed the decision of the appellate court.

Holding of the Supreme Court: Affirmed

Reasoning

Everson and other cases have shown that the line between state neutrality to religion and state support of religion is not easy to locate. "The constitutional standard is the separation of Church and State. The problem, like many problems in constitutional law, is one of degree." (*Zorach v. Clauson,* 343 U.S. 306.) From *Everson* comes this test: What are the purpose and the primary effect of the enactment? If either is the advancement or inhibition of religion then the enactment exceeds the scope of legislative power as circumscribed by the Constitution. That is to say that to withstand the strictures of the Establishment Clause there must be a secular legislative purpose and a primary effect that neither advances nor inhibits religion. That was the test in *Everson;* we reach the same result with respect to the New York law requiring school books to be loaned free of charge to all students in specified grades. Of course, books are different from buses. Most bus rides have no inherent religious significance, while religious books are common. However, the language of the law does not authorize the loan of religious books, and the state claims no right to distribute religious literature. Each book loaned must be approved by the public school authorities; only secular books may receive approval. In judging the validity of the statute on this record we must proceed on the assumption that books loaned to students are books that are not unsuitable for use in the public schools because of religious content.

Significance

The "child benefit" theory was strengthened and extended to another state, this time New York. The benefit is not to the school nor to the parents, but to the child who attends the school. As in *Cochran* (1930) the Court again said: "The State's interest is education, broadly; its method, comprehensive. Individual interests are aided only as the common interest is safeguarded." Private education must be recognized as playing a significant part in raising national levels of knowledge, competence and experience. Americans care about the quality of the secular education available to their children. Parochial schools are performing a valuable service in providing secular education to their students. Such an arrangement is not a law respecting an establishment of religion within the meaning of the First Amendment.

CASE CITATION: *Board of Education of Central School District No. 1 v. Allen, 88 S.Ct. 1923 (N.Y. 1968)*

18   State's Right to Control Its Teaching Personnel

John Thomas Scopes was convicted in a lower court for teaching in the public schools a theory that man has descended from a lower form of animal life in contravention of the Tennessee Anti-Evolution Act, which prohibited such teaching in universities, normal schools, and other public schools of the state. The case was tried in Dayton, Tenn. in July of 1925, and became known as the "Monkey Trial." The ACLU offered to pay the costs of a test case of the anti-evolution statute, and Scopes was persuaded to serve as defendant. William Jennings Bryan, three times a presidential candidate, joined the state in upholding the act; Clarence Darrow, the country's foremost criminal lawyer, defended Scopes. This was the first American trial to be nationally broadcast and aroused enormous discussion and considerable heat. Fundamentalism and the literal truth of the Scriptures were pitted on the one hand against radicalism, agnosticism, and science on the other. It became one of the most famous of all American criminal trials.

Relief Sought: Writ of error seeking reversal of decision rendered by trial court.

Issue: Does the state have the right to prohibit the teaching of the theory which holds that man has developed from some pre-existing form of life such as an animal lower on the scale?

Holding of the Trial Court: For the State

Holding of the Supreme Court of Tennessee: Affirmed as to constitutionality of the act; reversed as to the fine of $100

Reasoning

Plaintiff in error was a teacher in the public schools of Rhea County. He was an employee of the state of Tennessee or of a municipal agency of the state. He was under contract with the state to work in an institution of the state. He had no right or privilege to serve the state except upon such terms as the state prescribed. His liberty, his privilege, his immunity to teach and to proclaim the theory of evolution, elsewhere than in the service of the state, was in no wise touched by this law.

The statute before us is not an exercise of the police power of the state undertaking to regulate the conduct and contracts of individuals in their dealings with each other. On the other hand, it is an act of the state as a corporation, a proprietor, an employer. It is a declaration of a master as to the character of the work the master's servant shall, or rather shall not, perform. In dealing with its employees engaged upon its own work, the state is not hampered by the limitations of section 8 of article 1 of the Tennessee Constitution, nor of the Fourteenth Amendment to the Constitution of the United States.

Significance

The Scopes trial a) polarized the country into two camps with respect to the theory of evolution, b) caused Scopes to leave teaching for a career in geology, c) resulted in the death of William Jennings Bryan shortly after the close of the trial, and d) produced an interpretation of academic freedom which read: "Those who work for the state do so not under their own conditions but under the conditions laid down by the state." This was the definition of academic freedom in public education for many years.

CASE CITATION: *Scopes v. State of Tennessee, 289 S.W. 363 (Tenn. 1927)*

AUTHOR'S COMMENTARY

John Thomas Scopes rejected the notoriety which came his way following the "Monkey Trial." Aided by a scholarship, Scopes studied geology at the University of Chicago, then went to Venezuela. In 1960, he returned to Dayton to attend the premier of the movie which was made from his legal adventures, *Inherit the Wind*. On retirement, he authored the book, *Center of the Storm,* published by Holt, Rinehart and Winston, which is an account of the trial as he saw it from his vantage point as defendant.

In 1968, the United States Supreme Court, in *Epperson v. State of Arkansas,* 393 U.S. 97, Ark. 1968, had before it the question of a similar law in that state which made it unlawful for a teacher in any state-supported school or university "to teach the theory or doctrine that mankind ascended or descended from a lower order of animals," or to use any textbook which contained this theory. Mrs. Epperson, a teacher in a high school in Little Rock, was uncertain whether or not to use a newly-adopted textbook containing a chapter setting forth the theory in question. By this time, only Arkansas, Mississippi, and Tennessee had such anti-evolution statutes on their books. There had been no record of any prosecutions in Arkansas under that statute. The teacher decided to test the constitutionality of the act in question.

Although agreeing with Mrs. Epperson's attorney that the statute was vague, the Court nonetheless struck down the statute on another ground, that of its conflict with "the constitutional prohibition of state laws respecting an establishment of religion or prohibiting the free exercise thereof." The error, said the Court, was that the Arkansas law "selects from the body of knowledge a particular segment which it proscribes for the sole reason that it is deemed in conflict with a particular religious doctrine; that is, with a particular interpretation of the Book of Genesis by a particular religious group."

Although the Arkansas law made no mention of "any theory that denies the story of the Divine Creation of man, as taught in the Bible," (the Tennessee law did so state), there can be no doubt that Arkansas has sought to prevent its teachers from discussing the theory of evolution because "it is contrary to the belief of some that the Book of Genesis must be the exclusive source of doctrine as to the origin of man." Such a narrow interpretation, said the Court, is in conflict with the First Amendment. "The vigilant protection of constitutional freedoms is nowhere more vital than in the community of American schools." (From *Shelton v. Tucker*, 364 U.S. 479, 1960.) The First Amendment "does not tolerate laws that cast a pall of orthodoxy over the classroom." (From *Keyishian v. Bd. of Regents*, 385 U.S. 589, N.Y., 1967.)

Mr. Justice Black concurred, but on the basis of the statute's vagueness. Wrote Black: "I am also not ready to hold that a person hired to teach school children takes with him into the classroom a constitutional right to teach sociological, economic, political or religious subjects that the school's managers do not want discussed. This Court has said that the rights of free speech 'while fundamental in our democratic society,' still do not mean that everyone with opinions or beliefs to express may address a group at any public place and at any time. Does academic freedom permit a teacher to breach his contractual agreement to teach only the subjects designated by the school authorities who hired him?

"However wise this Court may be or may become hereafter, it is doubtful that, sitting in Washington, it can successfully supervise and censor the curriculum of every public school in every hamlet and city in the United States. I doubt that our wisdom is so nearly infallible."

19 *State's Right to Control Teacher Conduct Not Connected with Alleged Subversive Activities*

A tenure teacher wrote a letter critical of the board of education. The letter, published in a newspaper, attacked the board's handling of a bond issue and its subsequent allocation of financial resources between the school's academic and athletic programs. The letter, in effect, criticized the superintendent's "flaunting" of the needs of academic teachers, overemphasizing athletics, and misrepresenting the purposes of the bond issue, among other things. The teacher was dismissed by the superintendent, and after a hearing the board affirmed the dismissal.

Relief Sought: Reinstatement by a teacher to his former position.

Issue: Is a teacher's letter considered by the board and published in a newspaper so detrimental to the best interests of the school as to warrant the teacher's dismissal?

Holding of the Trial Court: For the defendant school board

Holding of the Appellate Court: Affirmed

Holding of the United States Supreme Court: Reversed and remanded

Reasoning

A public employee does not relinquish any part of his First Amendment rights to freedom of speech, despite the fact that his statements are directed at his nominal superiors.

The statements made by the teacher have in no way materially interfered with the orderly operation of the schools or the district's business or with the proper performance of the teacher's duties.

Absent proof of false statements knowingly and recklessly made, a teacher may not be dismissed for exercising his right to speak on public issues.

Dismissal is a potent means of inhibiting freedom of speech. But the theory that public employment which may be denied altogether may be subjected to any conditions, regardless of how unreasonable, has been uniformly rejected (by this Court). We do not deem it either appropriate or feasible to attempt to lay down a general standard against which all (teachers') statements may be judged. Pickering's letter was greeted by everyone but its main target, the Board, with massive apathy and total disbelief. The statements are not *per se* libelous nor detrimental to the board or its work, and represent only an opinion on the part of Pickering on a matter that clearly concerns an issue of general public interest. Free and open debate is vital to informed decision-making on such issues by the electorate. Accordingly, it is essential that they be able to speak out freely on such questions without fear of retaliatory dismissal.

Significance

Teachers are not second class citizens. They have a right, indeed a duty, to speak out on public issues even though they may be in disagreement with their employers, the board of education and the administration of the schools.

CASE CITATION: *Pickering v. Board of Education of Township High School District 205, 391 U.S. 563 (Ill. 1968)*

AUTHOR'S COMMENTARY

The *Pickering* decision will no doubt account for some changes in the principles of law surrounding the dismissal of teachers for critical remarks made against their employing boards of education. Following the 1968 decision, the Supreme Court vacated two such decisions made by the highest courts in the States of New York and Alaska. In *Puentes v. Board of Education,* 250 N.E.2d 232 (N.Y. 1969), the case was remanded for further consideration not inconsistent with the *Pickering* holding, and in *Watts v.*

Seward School Board, 454 P.2d 732 (Alaska 1969), the original judgment of the Supreme Court of Alaska was allowed to stand.

Thus, the principle of law with respect to teachers who publicly criticize the board of education, absent proof of false statements knowingly or recklessly made by them, is that teachers have the right to speak out on issues of public importance and such speaking-out shall not constitute the basis for their dismissal from public employment. While this does not mean that teachers have full and unbridled rights to criticize the board of education, it goes far indeed in the direction of saying that teachers are no longer second-class citizens within the earlier meaning of that word.

This latter principle seems to be expressed best in the words of the Supreme Court:

> The amounts expended on athletics which Pickering reported erroneously were matters of public record on which his position as a teacher in the district did not qualify him to speak with any greater authority than any other taxpayer. The Board could easily have rebutted his errors by publishing the accurate figures itself, either via a letter to the same newspaper or otherwise. . . . His statements have not been shown to have either impeded the teacher's proper performance of his daily duties in the classroom or to have interfered with the regular operation of the schools generally. In these circumstances we conclude that the interest of the school administration in limiting teachers' opportunities to contribute to public debate is not significantly greater than its interest in limiting a similar contribution by any member of the general public. . . . Judgment reversed and case remanded with directions.

20   *State's Right to Control Juvenile Offenders*

Parents of a 15-year-old boy petitioned for his release from a state industrial school to which he had been sentenced as a delinquent after a complaint by a neighbor, Mrs. Cook, following a telephone call to her home. Parents contended the boy had been denied due process in the juvenile court hearings leading up to his commitment, in that adequate notice of the charges, representation by counsel, confrontation by Mrs. Cook, sworn testimony, and the right to appeal had been denied him. The juvenile judge and probation officer testified at the habeas corpus trial that they were acting in the boy's best interests and that the right of appeal was prohibited under the Arizona state juvenile code. The county and State Supreme Courts dismissed the complaint and the parents appealed to the United States Supreme Court.

Relief Sought: Writ of habeas corpus to secure release of a juvenile from the state industrial school.

Issue: What are the rights to due process of a minor under a state's juvenile court code?

Holding of the trial court: Dismissed

Holding of the Appellate Court: Affirmed

Holding of the United States Supreme Court: Reversed

Reasoning

Due process does not allow a hearing to be held in which a youth's freedom and a parent's right to custody are at stake without giving them timely notice in advance of the juvenile court hearing listing the specific issues involved. Further, Mrs. Gault's knowledge that she could have counsel does not relieve the juvenile officers from informing her of this and providing it, if necessary. The informal nature of the proceedings in no way precluded the observance of the rights of confrontation by complainant, self-incrimination notice, and the right of cross-examination. The denial of such rights under the Arizona code is unconstitutional. Secrecy, as in Star Chamber proceedings, while intended to be beneficial to the child, denies him due process of law and violates the integrity of the individual's will.

The right to due process is not for adults alone.

Significance

The Constitution guarantees the right of due process and equal protection of the laws to all citizens, be they young or old. The state's role as *parens patriae* evolves from benevolent parent to fair and objective dispenser of justice. A new, state/juvenile relationship based on constitutional rights arose and re-evaluation of the procedures used in the juvenile court system throughout the country was undertaken.

CASE CITATION: *In the Matter of Gault, 87 S.Ct. 1428 (Ariz. 1967)*

AUTHOR'S COMMENTARY

As early as 1948, the United States Supreme Court had begun the series of cases leading to *Gault,* with a decision that "the constitution is not for adults alone." In *Haley v. Ohio,* 331 U.S. 596, 1966, Justice Douglas said, "Neither man nor child can be allowed to stand condemned by methods which flout constitutional requirements of due process of law." He was writing here about the provision of counsel and support for a juvenile when facing accusation. In *Gallegos v. Colorado,* 370 U.S. 49, 1962, a similar ruling pointed to the implication that neither the Fourteenth Amendment nor the Bill of Rights "is for adults alone." Then *Kent v. United States,* 383 U.S. 541, 1966 laid the groundwork for the *Gault* decision that juveniles must be afforded their constitutional rights which are no more nor less than those ordinarily accorded to adults.

In *Kent,* Justice Fortas wrote:

> The admonition to function in a 'parental' relationship is not an invitation to procedural arbitrariness. . . . We do not mean . . . to indicate that the hearing to be held must conform with all of the requirements of a criminal trial or even of the usual administrative hearing, but we do hold that the hearing must measure up to the essentials of due process and fair treatment.

While the *Kent* decision was fairly explicit, the *Gault* decision was more far-reaching. Covering some twenty-five pages, the opinion can be summarized in the words of Justice Fortas:

> We conclude that the constitutional privilege against self-incrimination is applicable in the case of juveniles as it is with respect to adults. We appreciate that special problems may arise with respect to waiver of the privilege by or on behalf of children and that there may well be some differences in techniques—but not in principle—depending upon the age of the child and the presence and competence of parents. The participation of counsel will, of course, assist the police, juvenile courts and appellate tribunals in administering the privilege. If counsel is not present for some permissible reason when an admission is obtained, the greatest care must be taken to assure that the admission is voluntary, in the sense that it is not the product of ignorance of rights or of adolescent fantasy, fright, or despair.

Prior to the *Gault* decision, the President's Crime Commission recommended that ". . . in order to assure procedural justice for the child, it is necessary that counsel . . . be appointed as a matter of course wherever coercive action is a possibility without requiring any affirmative choice by child or parent."

As a rule of thumb, the greater the offense with which a juvenile is charged in a school situation, the greater must be the attempt on the part of school officials to assure that he will receive due process of law as a constitutional right. It is not necessary to have counsel present in the exploration of lesser student offenses. As Lawrence W. Knowles noted at 4, *Journal of Family Law,* 172, 1964:

> Lesser student offenses may be treated differently. A student suspected of a violation of school regulations, but not a criminal offense, may be questioned with slightly greater latitude than a student suspected of a crime. It would not be necessary for a lawyer or the child's parents to be notified and permitted an opportunity to be present. However, if the suspected violation is one requiring expulsion, the school official should advise the student that he may remain silent if he so wishes. The reason for warning a student that he may remain silent rests on a comparison between expulsion from school and a criminal court proceeding. Both are punishments, and the student has some constitutional safeguards against punishments meted out by the state. One of these safeguards would seem to be the privilege against self-incrimination. If this is true, then the student must be counselled as regards this privilege, and such counselling would take the form of a warning by the school principal that the student need not supply answers which may form a basis for expelling him.

The juvenile court system is based on the principle of *parens patriae,* which is defined as the sovereign power of the state to guardianship over persons under disability. Unwilling to see children stand trial in adult courts, early reformers urged the creation of new courts for juveniles which would be attuned to their needs, and which would keep them separated from hardened criminals. Thus, *parens patriae* established the concept that the child, unlike an adult, has a right "not to liberty, but to custody." He can be made "to attorn to his parents, to go to school, and otherwise conduct himself in a lawful manner." If his parents fail to provide guidance for him— that is, if the child is "delinquent"—then the state may intervene. Though this process might deprive the child of some of his rights, nevertheless the ultimate benefits to be gained far outweighed the loss, at least, in theory. It was upon this line of reasoning that the juvenile court system arose.

However, in the *Gault* decision, the Court said:

> There is evidence . . . that there may be grounds for concern that the child (under this system) receives the worst of both worlds: that he gets neither the protections accorded adults nor the solicitous care and regenerative treatment postulated for children. . . . The constitutional and theoretical basis for this peculiar system is—to say the least—debatable.

Accordingly, following the *Gault* decision, juvenile courts were put on notice that they must afford defendants the essentials of due process in arriving at their decisions. Due process amounts to a notice of the charges before the time of the hearing, the right to counsel, right to confrontation and cross-examination of those appearing against the defendant, warning against self-incrimination, the right to a transcript of the proceedings, right to be considered innocent until proven guilty, and the right of appeal. In the final analysis, "due process" is nothing more nor less than the United States Supreme Court decides it is under the Fourteenth Amendment.

The *Gault* decision, along with other changes occurring in the society, may be changing the traditional concept of the principal's role standing *in loco parentis.* For example, when the principal is conducting an investigation, and a student remains silent when questioned about his part in the action, the student's silence may not be taken to mean that he is guilty, nor may the student be punished merely for exercising his right to remain silent. Another example involves occasions when the police visit the school to check out some civil or criminal activity locally. The principal's role ordinarily took into account the "greatest good to the greatest number," to the extent sometimes of removing the student who "got into trouble." The newer role which the principal now plays sees him as the advocate of the boy in trouble. His duty is not to the student body *per se,* but to the boy, and he is duty-bound to protect the constitutional rights of that boy and see that he is accorded all rights due him in full. Anything short of this standard of care will expose the principal to charges that he deprived a citizen of his constitutional rights, which, under the Civil Rights Act of 1871, is actionable in damages against the principal. (See *McLaughlin v. Tilendis,* 398 F.2d 287, Ill. 1968, Case No. 36.)

21 State's Right to Control Symbolic Speech of Students in Public Schools

In December, 1965 a group of students decided to wear black armbands during the holiday season to protest the war in Viet Nam. On December 15, 1965 the principals of the Des Moines schools adopted a policy that any student wearing such an armband in school who refused to remove it when asked would be suspended until he returned without the armband. Two days after the adoption of the rule, three students wore the armbands, Mary Beth Tinker, 13 years of age, her brother, John Tinker, 15, and another student. They were suspended on refusal to remove the armbands. They did not return to school until after New Year's day of 1966, the planned period for wearing the armbands. A complaint for an injunction was filed by their father.

    Relief Sought: Injunctive relief against enforcement of a school regulation prohibiting the wearing of black armbands in a public school.

    Issue: Is the wearing of a black armband in public school protected by the United States Constitution?

    Holding of the Trial Court: Case dismissed

    Holding of the Appellate Court: Court divided, writ of certiorari granted

    Holding of the United States Supreme Court: Reversed and remanded

Reasoning

Only a few of the 18,000 school children in the City of Des Moines wore the armbands and only five students in all were suspended for wearing them. There is no indication that the work of the school or any class was disrupted. The District Court concluded that the action of the school authorities was reasonable because it was based upon the fear of a disturbance from the wearing of the armbands. But in our system, undifferentiated fear or apprehension is not enough to overcome the right to freedom of expression. Any departure from absolute regimentation may cause trouble. Any variation from the majority's opinion may inspire fear. Any word spoken, in class, in the lunchroom or on the campus, that deviates from the views of another person, may start an argument or cause a disturbance. But our Constitution says we must take this risk. Our history says that it is this sort of hazardous freedom—this kind of openness—that is the basis of our national strength and of the independence and vigor of Americans who grow up and live in this relatively permissive, often disputatious society.

Significance

Absent a showing that the wearing of armbands would "materially and substantially interfere with the requirements of appropriate discipline in the operation of the school" such wearing of armbands cannot be prohibited on this basis alone. The prohibition of any particular symbol in schools, at least without evidence that it is necessary to avoid interference with school work or discipline, is not constitutionally permissible.

    CASE CITATION: *Tinker v. Des Moines School Board, 393 U.S. 503 (Iowa 1969)*

AUTHOR'S COMMENTARY

In the *Tinker* decision, the U.S. Supreme Court held that the wearing of armbands by students was symbolic speech akin to "pure speech" and therefore must be protected.

Under our Constitution, free speech is not a right that is given only to be so circumscribed that it exists in principle but not in fact. Freedom of expression would not truly exist if the right could be exercised only in an area that a benevolent government has provided as a safe haven for crackpots. The Constitution says that Congress (and the states) may not abridge the right to free speech. This provision means what it says. We properly read it to permit reasonable regulation of speech-connected activities in carefully restricted circumstances. But we do not confine the permissible exercise of First Amendment rights to a telephone booth or the four corners of a pamphlet, or to supervised or ordained discussion in a school classroom.

The Court, in arriving at its decision in *Tinker,* quoted from an earlier case, *Burnside v. Byars,* 363 F.2d 744, Miss. 1966, Case No. 48, *infra.* There students wore so-called "freedom buttons" in school and those who refused to remove them were suspended. The constitutional issue was the right of students to express opinions versus the right of local school authorities to establish reasonable rules in the operation of the schools. The federal district court held that the students had a right silently to communicate an idea and to encourage other children to do so in the exercise of their civil rights without fear of dismissal from school. In this case, there was no disruption of the on-going school program as a result of the wearing of the buttons.

However, in *Blackwell v. Issaquena County Board of Education,* 363 F.2d 749, (Miss. 1966) Case No. 49, *infra,* the same court upheld the suspension of some high school students for wearing freedom buttons when discourteous acts and a general disturbance disrupted the on-going program of the school. The nexus of the problem therefore seems to be whether the exercise of a constitutional right to expression interferes with the on-going program of the schools. If it does, it can be reasonably controlled, but not until *after* the disturbance has occurred, not before.

22   *State's Right to Expel College Students for Participating in Sit-In Demonstration*

Several students were involved in a sit-in demonstration in a privately-owned cafeteria in the basement of the Montgomery County Court House and in other peaceful civil rights demonstrations as well. On March 4, 1960, the plaintiffs were notified of their expulsion effective March 5, 1960 without notice of a hearing or appeal having been provided. No reason for their expulsion was given, but it was intimated that it was in the best interests of the college. The state further contended that there was no violation of due process since the students had been warned that if they were involved in any more demonstrations, severe action would be taken against them.

Relief Sought: Reinstatement to Alabama State University.

Issue: Are students who engage in sit-ins and are arrested entitled to a hearing before being expelled from a tax-supported college?

Holding of the Trial Court: For defendants, Alabama State Board of Education

Holding of the Appellate Court: Reversed and remanded

Reasoning

The right to attend a public college or university is not in and of itself a constitutional right. Students do not have a right to remain at a college or university if reasonable and constitutional grounds for expulsion can be shown. It is possible that a rule covering student conduct could be reasonable, and the penalty for breaking the rule also reasonable, but the procedure for determining whether the student had broken the rule could be unreasonable. The concept of due process is not precise, since the essential elements depend in each instance upon the peculiar set of circumstances attendant upon the case at hand. The right to an education at public expense is valuable. In general, before one can be deprived of this right, he must have had some opportunity to explain his behavior. The more extreme the possible penalty, the more entitled he is to protection of his rights. Expulsion is a very severe penalty, since it deprives the student of his opportunity to complete his education. Due process would include at least a legal hearing at which the student may face his accusers, may be represented by counsel, and may hear the charges against him. The right to counsel is not always required where the action is civil rather than criminal, and the other essential elements of due process are present.

Significance

The sit-in cases raised the issue of whether a student's relationship to his university or college is entirely one of contract alone, or whether there is not a constitutional right which must be recognized in the case in which the student is to be terminated. In state-supported colleges at least, students are entitled to "due process" before dismissal, although it is not always clear what this amounts to in each case. Due process must be determined in the circumstances surrounding each case, and no general rules are possible except to say that the procedure used must meet the general test of "fairness."

CASE CITATION: *Dixon v. Alabama State Board of Education, 186 F.Supp. 945, reversed 294 F.2d 150, Cert. denied, 368 U.S. 930 (Ala. 1961)*

AUTHOR'S COMMENTARY

Seven civil rights acts were passed by the Congress during the Reconstruction Period, 1866 to 1875. Aimed at liberating the Negro and giving him equal rights with whites, these acts were nullified by the Supreme Court in 1883 when the Court declared unconstitutional the parts (Secs. 1 & 2, Civil Rights Act of 1875) which afforded "persons of color" access to hotels, theaters, and restaurants. Denial of equal accommodations, said the Court, "imposes no badge of slavery" upon the persons affected; since the Thirteenth Amendment applies only to slavery, the Amendment is no source of power for the Congressional imposition of punishment for mere discriminatory practices. Also, the Fourteenth Amendment applies only to the states; Congress may therefore pass only laws affecting discrimination by the states and not by private citizens (109 U.S. 3, 1883). These cases, plus some eight others handed down by the Supreme Court following 1873, permitted the maintenance of segregation-discrimination patterns throughout the nation, despite the Thirteenth, Fourteenth, and Fifteenth Amendments. Not until the Civil Rights Act of 1957 did the Congress again speak to the problem of segregation of the races.

The logic of the lone dissenter, Justice John Marshall Harlan, was lost on the majority: "Constitutional provisions, adopted in the interest of liberty . . . have been so construed as to defeat the ends the people desire to accomplish." He followed it up in 1896 by dissenting in the *Plessy* decision, when he compared the *Plessy* decision with the *Dred Scott* decision using in part these words:

> The white race deems itself to be the dominant race in this country. . . . But in the view of the Constitution, in the eye of the law, there is in this country no superior, dominant, ruling class of citizens. There is no caste here. Our Constitution is color-blind, and neither knows nor tolerates classes among citizens. In respect of civil rights, all citizens are equal before the law. The humblest is the peer of the most powerful. The law regards man as man, and takes no account of his surroundings or of his color. . . . Sixty millions of whites are in no danger from the presence here of eight millions of blacks. The destinies of the two races, in this country, are indissolubly linked together. . . . What can more certainly arouse race hate, what can more certainly create and perpetuate a feeling of distrust between these races, than state enactments, which, in fact, proceed on the ground that colored citizens are so inferior and degraded that they cannot be allowed to sit

in public coaches occupied by white citizens? If the (Louisiana) law is allowed to stand, slavery as an institution tolerated by law would, it is true, have disappeared from our country, but there would remain a power in the States, by sinister legislation, to interfere with the full enjoyment of the blessings of freedom; to regulate civil rights, common to all citizens, upon the basis of race; and to place in a condition of legal inferiority a large body of American citizens, now constituting a part of the political community called the People of the United States. . . . For the reasons stated, I am constrained to withhold my assent from the opinion and judgment of the majority.

This was the condition of things in the South when the so-called "sit-in cases" took place between 1961 and 1964. The first interpretation on the sit-in problem arose for the Supreme Court in 1961, when the principal statement was made in *Garner v. Louisiana,* 368 U.S. 157, a case which set aside sit-in convictions based on breach of the peace statutes. In 1963, the Court again acted in *Peterson v. Greenville,* 373 U.S. 244, this time setting aside sit-in convictions based on criminal trespass statutes. In 1964, the Court again considered criminal trespass statutes in the case of *Bell v. Maryland,* 378 U.S. 226.

In refusing certiorari in *Dixon v. Alabama State Board of Education,* 186 F.Supp. 945, 1961, the Court was, in effect, upholding students who engage in sit-ins in right to due process of law (Case No. 22, *supra*). For this reason, and because the other sit-in cases were concerned with non-students, this case is of more than passing interest at this point.

The passage of the Twenty-fourth Amendment guaranteeing to citizens the right to vote in any primary or other election for President or Vice-president regardless of whether or not they had paid a poll tax, and the adoption of the Civil Rights Act of 1964 by the Congress, further strengthened the rights of minority groups in this country during the 1960's. But much still remains to be done before the problem of equal educational opportunities is finally put at rest.

PART TWO

Employee Negotiations
and Related Problems

Part Two

Employee Negotiations
and Related Problems

*P*rior to the passage of the Wagner Act by the Congress in 1935, public school teachers could be dismissed for membership in labor unions. Two such cases show the reasoning of the courts. In *People ex rel. Fursman v. City of Chicago,* 116 N.E. 158, Ill. 1917, the court upheld a board rule dismissing school employees in that city from the employ of the district. In the City of Chicago, 3,500 teachers were members of the Federation of Teachers, among them one Ida M. Fursman, who joined with other teachers similarly situated in testing the board resolution. The court *inter alia* had these thoughts concerning the legality of the board rule:

The board of education has the power to make and enforce any rules that it sees proper. The board has the absolute right to decline to employ or re-employ any applicant for a position as teacher for any or no reason. Membership by teachers in unions or in organizations of teachers affiliated with labor unions, or a federation or association of trade unions, is inimical to proper discipline, prejudicial to the efficiency of the teaching force and detrimental to the welfare of the school system. Therefore, such membership or affiliation is hereby prohibited. . . . No person has the right to demand that he or she shall be employed as a teacher. The board is the best judge of whether or not to employ or re-employ. The adoption of the rule under consideration was an exercise of the discretionary power of the board which courts cannot interfere with. Questions of policy are solely for the board, and when they have once been determined by it, we will not interfere to inquire into their propriety. The decree of the court below is reversed and the cause remanded with direction to dissolve the injunction and dismiss the bill.

71

Similarly, in *Seattle High School Chapter 200, AFT v. Sharples,* 293 Pac. 994, Wash. 1930, the court upheld a board rule forbidding membership by its teachers in a labor union on pain of dismissal. The resolution stipulated

> . . . that no person be employed hereafter, or continued in the employ of this district as a teacher while a member of the American Federation of Teachers, or any local thereof; and that before any election shall be considered binding, such teacher shall sign a declaration to the following effect:
>
> *I hereby declare that I am not a member of the American Federation of Teachers, or any local thereof, and will not become a member during the term of this contract.*

The court pointed out that by state statute the board of education is given complete control of the schools of the city. Among its powers are those of employing teachers and fixing their salaries. It is also empowered to enact such ordinances as it may deem necessary and expedient for the proper management of the schools. This does not interfere with the rights of the teacher, who can be dismissed for sufficient cause. The courts will not interfere with the parties since the exercise of the board's discretion is not controlled by the Fourteenth Amendment. Refusal to employ "is not a denial of a constitutional right of a person to follow his chosen profession."

However, following the passage of the Wagner Act, no more cases involving dismissal of teachers for union membership were tried. Now, union activity for the teacher, so long as it does not interfere with the teacher's job, is considered a protected constitutional guarantee. See Case No. 36, *infra.* The development of the idea, however, did not come about without considerable litigation, and is not considered to be settled law even today.

In 1939, for example, suit was brought in the Circuit Court of Illinois, Peoria branch, to restrain the board of education in that city from entering into or carrying out the terms of an agreement which the board had with its non-certificated employees. The contract in question was with the Firemen and Oilers Local 8-A, American Federation of Labor, and among other things, provided that all workers in the district in the capacity of janitors, firemen, engineers, ground keepers and janitresses should be and remain members in good standing of the said local union. While agreeing that the workers undoubtedly had the right to organize themselves into a union, the court nonetheless would not sanction the arrangement in question on the grounds that it was beyond the powers of a local governmental body to perform. *Chapin v. Board of Education of the City of Peoria,* Circuit Court of

Illinois, Peoria, Illinois, No. 21255, December 9, 1939. Said the court on that occasion:

> The question is whether the board of education has a right to enter into a combination with such an organization for the expenditure of the taxpayers' money for the benefit of members of the organization, and to exclude any portion of the citizens following lawful trades and occupations from the right to labor. It has no such right. . . .
>
> The board cannot, however, by contract, foreclose the possibility of a non-member securing employment. The law finds no fault with a school board employing union labor or with its employees belonging to labor unions, but it does not permit the board to bind itself by contract to employ only those who belong to a particular association or organization. In this respect, the contract is illegal and funds expended under and by virtue of such a contract would necessarily amount to an illegal expenditure of public funds, and a taxpayer may maintain a suit for an injunction.

This second section of the present volume is designed to assist the school administrator, student, teacher, or school board member to understand the development of the common law which arose in connection with collective bargaining for teachers. It begins with the most influential case of this kind, the "grandfather" of all collective bargaining cases in public education, the "Norwalk" case of 1951, which became the model for later litigation in the absence of a statute on collective bargaining for teachers. The fifties were relatively quiet, however, and it was not until the sixties that litigation involving public school teachers became prominent. The fourteen cases in this section range in time from 1951 to 1969, and involve eleven states from Connecticut to Washington. They show that collective bargaining for teachers is chiefly a common law rather than a statutory proposition; even in those states having statutes on the subject, the courts still continue to interpret the meanings of the statutes, and in the process, often resort to their earlier decisions in reaching a conclusion on the questions at hand.

23   Collective Bargaining for Teachers

The Norwalk Teachers' Association represented 298 out of 300 teachers employed in the City of Norwalk. In April 1946 there was a dispute over salaries. Some teachers turned down their respective contracts and refused to return to work. Some of them were thereupon dismissed. After negotiations, the teachers returned to work under contracts which were subject to the conditions to be set forth in the court's decision. The questions posed by the parties related to teachers' rights to organize as a labor union, to use the strike and other work stoppage to enforce their demands, to enter into written agreements with their board of education, and to mediate and arbitrate disputes.

Relief Sought: Adjudication of its legal position and right to bargain by an organization of public school teachers

Issue: May teachers organize and engage in concerted action in the form of a strike or collective refusal to enter upon their teaching duties?

Holding of the Trial Court: Certain questions were reserved for the advice of the Supreme Court of Errors

Holding of the Appellate Court: Rendered declaratory judgment, with no costs to either party

Reasoning

Held: teachers may legally organize as a union to bargain collectively with the board of education. But this right is qualified, i.e., they may not organize where the purpose is to strike if demands are not met, but they may organize to negotiate. Since the State does not preclude the right of school boards to recognize a teachers' union, recognition is permissible. Negotiations by some representative is the most common way teachers' desires may be presented, and is permissible if it does not include a strike threat. The courts have in the past uniformly enjoined the right of teachers to strike. They do not have such a legal right (to strike). A city and any other unit of government may enter into an agreement with a union to arbitrate, so long as the arbitration would decide questions of liability and not questions of policy. A school board may not delegate its broad policy-making power. Teachers serve the public welfare. To say that they can strike is the equivalent of saying that they can deny the authority of the government and disregard the public welfare. The government is established and run for all of the people, not for the benefit of any person or group. The profit motive, inherent in the free enterprise system, is absent. It should be the aim of every employee of government to do his or her part to make it function as efficiently and economically as possible. The drastic remedy of the organized strike to enforce the demands of unions of government employees is in direct contravention to this principle, and cannot be allowed.

Significance

Teachers may legally organize and approach their school boards in a spirit of bargaining. Boards may enter into such negotiations with teachers but may not abrogate their responsibility to have the last word. The strike by governmental employees is prohibited, since these employees are agents of the government and as such occupy a status entirely different from workers in the private sector of the economy. Any action to strike against the government can be considered treasonable.

CASE CITATION: *Norwalk Teachers' Association v. Board of Education of City of Norwalk, 83 A.2d 482 (Conn. 1951)*

AUTHOR'S COMMENTARY

In the *Norwalk* case, the court in denying public employees the right to strike, quoted with approval from statements of three former Presidents:

There is no right to strike against public safety by anybody anywhere at any time.—Calvin Coolidge

The strike (by public employees) is an intolerable crime against civilization.—Woodrow Wilson

Particularly, I want to emphasize my conviction that militant tactics have no place in the functions of any organization of Government employees. . . . A strike of public employees manifests nothing less than an intent on their part to prevent or obstruct the operations of Government until their demands are satisfied. Such action, looking toward the paralysis of Government by those who have sworn to support it, is unthinkable and intolerable.—Franklin D. Roosevelt

Legislation in some states in 1970 gave public school teachers "the right to join or not to join any organization or professional or economic improvement association without prejudice," although the majority of the states were still uncommitted on this right. However, the First Amendment right of the people "peaceably to assemble, and to petition the government for a redress of grievances" implies the right of citizens to join or not to join organizations of their own choosing.

The courts are divided on the question of whether a private school faculty is included under the state's labor relations act. In *Industrial Commission of Colorado v. Wallace Village for Children*, 437 P.2d 62, Colo. 1968, for example, the faculty of a non-profit school for minimally brain damaged children claimed to the state agency which handles industrial disputes that their employer had refused to bargain collectively with their union. After a hearing, the Industrial Commission filed a complaint against the private school, seeking a determination of its position.

The trial court held for the plaintiffs, but the Colorado Supreme Court, by a five to four vote, reversed the lower court on the grounds that the state's Labor Peace Act does not specify that it applies only to industry and trade. Therefore, because it applies to all industries and occupations, said the court, it applies to Wallace Village school. In its holding here, the Colorado Supreme Court refused to overthrow its earlier decision in *St. Luke's Hospital v. Industrial Commission of Colorado,* 142 Colo. 28, 349 P.2d 995, wherein the hospital had been exempted from the labor peace act provisions because it was a private *charitable* hospital, a distinction which it denied the Wallace Village school.

24   *Union Shop for Teachers*

An agreement entered into between a school board and a teachers' union contained a provision that any non-tenured teacher who failed to join the union within thirty days would be discharged upon the written request of the union, and any tenured teacher who refused to join the union would receive none of the benefits or salary increases negotiated by the union. Eight tenured teachers who were not members of the union and who had been denied salary increases under the agreement sued to obtain salary increases accorded to other teachers who had joined the union. Before returning their contracts, they had deleted the provisions requiring them to become members of the union. Their salaries, however, were $300 per year less than those provided for in the master agreement between the board and the union.

Relief Sought: Mandamus to compel the board to provide salary equal to other teachers, and to issue contracts to eight tenure teachers

Issue: May a school district require union membership of teachers in order for them to receive increases in salary?

Holding of the Trial Court: For the plaintiffs

Holding of the Supreme Court of Montana: Affirmed

Reasoning

The security clause (on union shop) is void and illegal. The board may not require union membership as a condition of employment because the legislature has not given it this power. The board may not discriminate between teachers employed by it as to the amount of salary paid to each on the basis of membership or non-membership in a labor union. Plaintiffs could not sue in contract for the increased salaries because they had no written contract, and therefore had no plain, speedy or adequate remedy in ordinary course of law. Even though their contracts were void, the teachers (plaintiffs) were entitled to be treated, for salary purposes, the same as other teachers in the district, and were entitled to recover from the defendant district the costs of their attorneys' fees.

Significance

A school district has no authority to discriminate between teachers employed by it as to the amount of salary paid because of membership, or non-membership, in a labor union.

For a governmental agency, such as a local board of education, which is representative of all the taxpayers, to enter into a contract favoring those who join unions over those who do not, was here held to be a discrimination between different classes of citizens, and therefore illegal and void in its entirety.

CASE CITATION: *Benson v. School District No. 1 of Silver Bow County, 344 P.2d 117 (Mont. 1959)*

AUTHOR'S COMMENTARY

A favorite "union security clause" among labor unions is the one which requires an employee within a specified length of time to join the union or be fired. This so-called "union shop clause" was restricted by the Congress in the Taft-Hartley Act in 1947. In *Benson,* the question for the court was whether the board of education was acting outside its powers in entering into an agreement to honor the union shop in governmental employment. The court said that the board was indeed acting in this way.

Said the court:

> Unlike a private corporation, the public corporation has limited power only. It has only such powers as are given to it by law and as are necessarily implied from those granted, and no others. . . . For the purposes of this case it is sufficient to say that the School Trustees have no authority or power to discriminate between the teachers employed by it as to the amount of salary paid to each because of their membership or lack of membership in a labor union. The School Trustees have no authority to invade that field. As well might it be argued that the Board of Trustees might provide that the increased salary shall not be allowed to those who do not affiliate with a certain lodge, service club, church or political party.

As a matter of law, the government is the property of all citizens, and every citizen should have an equal opportunity to work for the government, unhindered by intervening board restrictions related to membership in a labor organization. To require the worker to join an organization, said the court, is discriminatory, and must be prohibited in the interest of fair play for all citizens.

Curiously, in *Benson* the written agreement with the union prohibited the board from hiring married women as teachers unless they were already on tenure, in which event they also would be denied salary increases. None of the eight plaintiffs made a point of challenging this provision of the agreement, although it was a discrimination against married women. Today, it would be in violation of the Civil Rights Act of 1964, which prohibits discrimination in employment on account of the sex of the worker.

25   *Right to Membership or Non-Membership in Professional Organizations*

Plaintiff teacher was not given tenure and challenged the board's right to fail to re-employ him without giving him a hearing. On the second claim, he challenged the validity of a board rule which read: "Each person on this salary schedule shall join the professional organizations which include the community Teachers' Association, the National Education Association, the Missouri State Teachers' Association, and the St. Louis Suburban Teachers' Association. Failure to join such associations precludes the benefits derived through the salary schedule and places such person outside the salary schedule." Plaintiff sought an injunction against the enforcement of the rule, and an award of his dues paid in protest to these associations.

Relief Sought: Injunctive relief from a board rule requiring teachers to join certain professional organizations

Issue: May the school board require teachers to join professional organizations on failure of which they will be precluded from the benefits derived through the salary schedule?

Holding of the Trial Court: Sustained defendant's motion to dismiss

Holding of the Appellate Court: Affirmed in part; reversed in part

Reasoning

The court upheld the board rule, saying that it had the legal right to adopt the rule in question, as well as "other needful rules and regulations for the organization, grading and government in their school district." The court also ruled that, having accepted the salary according to the schedules during his employment in the school district, the teacher could not recover the amount of the dues he paid to the local education associations. Said the court: "In the teaching profession, as in all professions, membership in professional organizations tends to improve the interest, knowledge, experience and overall professional competence of the teacher. Membership in professional organizations is no guaranty of professional excellence, but active participation in such organizations, attendance at meetings where leaders give the members the benefit of their experience and where mutual problems and experiences and practices are discussed, are reasonably related to development of higher professional attainments and qualifications." In noting the difference between this case and *Benson* (see Case No. 24, *supra*) the court said: "Union membership *per se* has no connection with teaching competence. Plaintiff Magenheim was not *required* to meet the conditions stated in Paragraph 15 and 18 of the Salary Schedules. Teachers employed by defendant district who do not choose to meet the conditions stated for compensation under the Salary Schedules will have an individually negotiated compensation."

Significance

Apparently, the board of education, in the absence of prohibitory statutes to the contrary, may require organizational membership as a condition of moving up on the salary scale. But it may not require such membership as a condition of continuing employment in the district. (Distinguish *Benson, supra*.)

CASE CITATION: *Magenheim v. Board of Education of Riverview Gardens, 347 S.W.2d 409 (Mo. 1961)*

26   Right of Teachers "to Petition the Government for a Redress of Grievances"

Thirty-one individual teachers comprising the officers and board of the Secondary Teachers' Association of New York City sought to have the law which declared strikes by employees of the state ruled unconstitutional. Michael Pruzan and others proposed to go *en masse* to Albany to consult with the executive and legislative branches of the state government about working conditions and benefits for teachers, as well as the educational standards in the secondary schools in New York City. They raised the question of the applicability of the act: did it prevent the exercise of the First Amendment's right to petition the government for a redress of grievances, since legislative sessions occur only during school hours?

> *Relief Sought:* Declaratory judgment that the Condon-Wadlin Act was unconstitutional

Issue: May teachers absent themselves from their jobs during school hours in order to petition the government for a redress of grievances?

Holding of the Trial Court: For defendant

Holding of the Appellate Court: Affirmed

Reasoning

There is a superior interest by the state in an uninterrupted educational system to the right to petition. The committees of the legislature also hold hearings, as well as individual legislators being available during times and places which would present no conflict with teachers' obligations. But the court did add that it felt the law in question was "too severe and restrictive" and "unreasonably restrictive" in not allowing for "approved leaves of absences . . . for purposes set forth in the complaint." The statute is constitutional. Ordinarily the courts do not make hypothetical adjudications in the absence of a genuine justiciable controversy; however, teachers are entitled to know whether their planned absences would cost them their jobs. A judgment was desirable also because in the public interest there seemed to be doubts about the act's constitutionality on a widespread scale. The statute does provide for a hearing, and the definition of a strike (any failure to perform) as contained in the statute is as clear and definite as any definition can reasonably be. The statute provides only that they may not be absent from work to exercise the rights of free speech, assembly and right to petition but does not deny them these rights. The statute is therefore constitutional.

Significance

This was one of numerous attempts by teachers' groups to knock down the Condon-Wadlin Act, but the courts upheld it as a reasonable exercise of the state's right to protect the public welfare. The rights of teachers to First Amendment guarantees must be protected, but they must yield when they conflict with a higher public interest. The public interest in an uninterrupted public educational system is highly prized.

CASE CITATION: *Pruzan v. Board of Education of City of New York, 209 N.Y.S.2d 966 (N.Y. 1960)*

27   *Rights of Teachers' Organizations to Have Dues Withheld*

The petitioners, McGlaughlin and others, were acting on behalf of themselves and at least 75 others who belonged to the local teachers' union.

They sought to have their dues in the Niagara Falls Federation of Teachers, affiliated with the AFT, AFL-CIO, deducted from their salaries by the school board. The Board refused to do this, although it was already providing this service for the rival majority association.

Relief Sought: Union rights to deduction of membership dues from salaries

Issue: Can the union, as a minority organization, require the board to withhold union dues from their salaries, where the board has provided this service to the competing majority professional association?

Holding of the Trial Court: In favor of respondent, the Niagara Falls Board of Education

Holding of the Appellate Court: Affirmed

Reasoning

Under the General Municipal Law, municipal corporations or political subdivisions of the state are "authorized" on written request of an employee to deduct from his salary membership dues in a duly organized association or organization of civil service employees. The teachers contend that this provision is mandatory, while the board argues that it is permissive and discretionary.

The court held that the word *authorized* as used in the statute gave the board discretionary power to deduct dues, but did not require it to do so. In defining the word authorize as "to clothe with authority or legal power; to give a right to act," the court pointed out that in rulings by the state comptroller and court decisions, the word had been construed as discretionary and permissive, rather than mandatory in nature.

Significance

Depending upon the state's statutes, the board may or may not be required to withhold union dues; the state statutes should be checked in each instance to determine the attitude of the law on this point. Where there is a statute on a given question, the courts will attempt to interpret the intent of the legislature in making it; where no law exists, the common law (*stare decisis*) will control.

Generally, an authorization will be mandatory where the act authorized concerns public interest or the rights of individuals, but the making of deductions at the request of an employee "involves neither public interest nor private rights and is merely a convenience."

CASE CITATION: *McGlaughlin v. Niagara Falls Board of Education, 237 N.Y.S.2d 761 (N.Y. 1963)*

28   *Public Employees' Right to Collective Bargaining Benefits*

Plaintiffs were an association of employees who were performing custodial tasks for the Board of Education of the City of Wichita. The majority of the district's employees in this classification were members of the association. The members obtained a union charter from an industrial union sanctioned by the AFL-CIO. In June 1962, plaintiffs filed a petition with the State Labor Commissioner requesting that he call an election to determine the proper bargaining unit under Kansas law. The commissioner informed the plaintiff that, in his opinion and that of the attorney general, he could not legally call an election because the board of education was not an "employer" within the meaning of the state's labor relations act.

Relief Sought: Writ of mandamus to require holding of an election to determine the appropriate bargaining unit

Issue: Is the Board of Education of the City of Wichita an "employer" within the meaning of the state's labor relations statute?

Holding of the Trial Court: For the defendant

Holding of the Appellate Court: Affirmed

Reasoning

The school district is an arm of the state existing only as a creature of the legislature to operate as a political subdivision of the state. A school district has only such power and authority as is granted to it by the legislature and its power to contract, including contracts for employment, is only such as is conferred either expressly or by necessary implications. The general rule recognized in this jurisdiction, that statutes limiting rights or interests will not be interpreted to include the sovereign power unless it be expressly named or intended by necessary implication . . . applies to statutes limiting the power to control compensation, terms and conditions of employment. . . . We find nothing to indicate that the legislature intended to embrace political subdivisions in the term "employer" as used in the act, and thus make political subdivisions and governmental agencies subject to the labor laws of the state including collective bargaining. Since the board was not an "employer" within the meaning of the act, the state labor commissioner was without authority to conduct an election to determine a collective bargaining unit for the district's employees. Mandamus will not lie to compel the performance of an unauthorized act on the part of a public official.

Significance

State labor relations acts in general apply only to workers in the private sector of the economy and unless the language clearly shows that public employees are to be included under its provisions, the statute will not apply to them or to their activities in the collective bargaining field.

CASE CITATION: *Wichita Public Schools Employees' Union Local v. Smith, 397 P.2d 357 (Kans. 1964)*

AUTHOR'S COMMENTARY

It was the intent of the legislative bodies of the states to include only employees of private and "non-charitable" industrial and business firms under the state's labor relations statutes, denying to public employees collective bargaining rights long recognized as essential to labor union peace. In this respect, the collective bargaining rights of public employees have lagged some three decades behind those of workers in the private sector of the economy.

As we noted under Case No. 23, Author's Commentary, *supra,* a private school faculty may come within the provisions of the state's labor relations act, if it is adjudicated that the institution for which they work is not a "charitable" institution. See *Industrial Commission of Colorado v. Wallace Village for Children*, 437 P.2d 62, Colo. 1968; *contra. St. Luke's Hospital v. Industrial Commission of Colorado,* 349 P.2d 995, Colo.

Since public employees are ordinarily excluded from collective bargaining, the states are operating under one of four types of situations: 1) a state law "permits" the public employer to bargain with its employees; 2) a state law "mandates" that the public employer must bargain with its employees; 3) a state law allows employees "to present proposals" regarding wages, hours and working conditions; and 4) there is a complete absence of state law regarding collective bargaining for public employees. By January 1, 1970, twenty-three states had statutes of either the 1, 2, or 3 variety, while 27 states had no enabling legislation for public employees. The trend seemed to be toward more states enacting such legislation, however.

29   *Public Employees' Right to Conduct Strikes and Picket*

Named defendants were thirteen members of the union who had been custodial employees of the board of education. On August 3, 1964, union officers presented to the board a proposed collective bargaining agreement on behalf of the 13 employees of the Teamsters, Chauffeurs and Helpers union, but the board refused to sign the agreement for various reasons. On September 2, 1964, a regularly scheduled school day, the thirteen custodial employees did not report for work, but with the help of the union set up picket lines at each of the seven schools in the district. The picketing was peaceful, and there was no showing that any of the defendants coerced or advised any persons not to cross the picket lines. During the next eight days, normal school operations were disrupted as follows: (1) attendance figures were low; (2) milk and bread deliveries to the schools were not made when deliverymen refused to cross the picket lines; (3) schools were not cleaned; (4) the employees of a roofing contractor refused to cross the picket lines to repair a leaky roof; (5) transportation of pupils was affected; and (6) the board closed the schools completely from September 8 through 10th. Schools opened again on the 11th, but volunteers were used to clean the buildings, no hot water was available for showers, and other school personnel were forced to perform janitorial duties.

Relief Sought: Injunctive relief to restrain custodial employees from conducting a strike against the schools and from picketing in support of the strike

Issue: May public school employees strike against their governing boards and picket in support of such a strike?

Holding of the Trial Court: For defendants

Holding of the Supreme Court of Illinois: Reversed and remanded with directions

Reasoning

There is no inherent right in municipal employees to strike against their governmental employers. Teachers (and other employees) are agents of the state government and as such exercise a portion of the sovereign power of the state. It has been generally held that persons exercising a portion of the sovereign power of the state government have no right to strike against the government. Picketing is more than free speech because picket lines are designed to exert, and do exert, influences which produce actions and consequences different from other modes of communication. Picketing may be restrained where it is for an unlawful purpose under state laws or policies. (Quoting from Justice Frankfurter: It has been amply recognized that picketing, not being the equivalent of speech as a matter of fact, is not its inevitable legal equivalent. Picketing is not beyond the control of a state if the manner in which picketing is conducted or the purpose which it seeks to effectuate gives ground for its disallowance.)

Significance

Picketing, even though peaceful, may be restrained (enjoined) where the picketing is for an unlawful purpose or to impede or obstruct a vital and important governmental function—the proper and efficient education of our children—making its curtailment necessary "to protect the patently over-riding public interest."

CASE CITATION: *Board of Education of Community Unit School District No. 2 v. Redding, 207 N.E.2d 427 (Ill. 1965)*

30 *Teacher Involvement in Organizational Activities*

Frank Yuen was a tenured physical education teacher in Kane County, Illinois. He was vice-president of the Elgin Teachers' Association. He had requested permission to be absent on two days of school to attend a hearing of the Illinois School Problems Commission and a meeting of the National Department of Classroom Teachers. His initial request was denied because the meetings were not "related to physical education" and no substitutes were available. His second request was likewise denied. Nevertheless, he absented himself and attended the meetings in question. He was dismissed as a teacher after which he brought suit to be reinstated to his position as teacher.

Relief Sought: Reinstatement to his position as a teacher

Issue: Can organizational activities be allowed to interfere with a teacher's duties under the contract, and is the superintendent's refusal to allow the teacher to attend a professional meeting an invasion of the teacher's rights?

Holding of the Trial Court: Judgment for the plaintiff; Yuen reinstated as a teacher and sum of $7,500 granted to him

Holding of the Appellate Court: Reversed and remanded

Reasoning

An individual teacher signs a personal performance contract and a substitute will not suffice if the teacher is in good health and can reasonably be expected to be in the classroom teaching. When Yuen willfully absented himself from the school, he denied the benefit of his teaching to 160 to 175 children on that day. The Board of Education found that the loss to the students from Yuen's absence and his intentional violation of a ruling of the Board were not remedial. Once the willful violation occurred the damage was done and could not be remedied. This finding is not contrary to the manifest weight of the evidence. Under the Teacher Tenure Act, the board is the trier of the facts. The authority of the board cannot be interfered with by the courts unless it is justified in cases where the board has acted maliciously, capriciously or arbitrarily. It was a fair dismissal and the teacher is not entitled to a warning prior to the discharge.

Significance

A teacher's outside activities cannot be allowed to interfere with his duties as a teacher, especially after he has been denied permission to attend to such outside activities. Teachers work under personal performance contracts, and the law does not recognize substitutes to do their work when they are well and personally able to perform it themselves. Absenting oneself from work when denied permission to be absent for a particular purpose amounts to insubordination and if the teacher is later dismissed, he cannot be heard to complain.

CASE CITATION: *Yuen v. Board of Education of School District No. U-46, 222 N.E.2d 570 (Ill. 1966)*

31   *Collective Bargaining as a Constitutional Right*

Indiana was without a law requiring school boards to bargain collectively with exclusive representatives of teachers. Nevertheless, school boards in Indiana traditionally held informal negotiating sessions with teachers. The Indianapolis Board of Education agreed to hold a representative election to determine the teachers' exclusive representative agent for purposes of entering into negotiations. On the eve of the election, the Board unilaterally adopted a salary schedule and sent out individual teacher contracts. Claiming this action on the part of the board constituted a lack of good faith, the Indianapolis Education Association sought and obtained a federal injunction under the Civil Rights Act of 1871. Here the question of its validity is being tried.

Relief Sought: To enjoin the board from bargaining individually with teachers and to bargain only with the elected representative of the teachers.

Issue: In the absence of a statute, does the board have a constitutional duty to bargain with an exclusive bargaining agent?

Holding of the United States District Court: Issued injunctive relief

Holding of the United States Court of Appeals: Reversed

Reasoning

There is no question that the right of teachers to associate for the purpose of collective bargaining is a right protected by the First and Fourteenth Amendments to the Constitution. Nothing in this order is meant in any way to dilute this proposition. Nor can it be doubted that actions under color of law which infringe upon this fundamental right may be properly enjoined by a federal court. The factual allegations of the complaint, however, do not support allegations that First and Fourteenth Amendment rights of the teachers' group were violated by the board. Rather, the acts which are here complained of were rendered moot by the election and operation of the Association. *There is no constitutional duty to bargain collectively with an exclusive bargaining agent. Such duty, when imposed, is imposed by statute.* The refusal of the board to bargain in good faith does not equal a constitutional violation of the Association's positive rights of association, free speech, petition, equal protection, or due process. Nor does the fact that the agreement to bargain collectively may be enforceable against a state elevate a contractual right to a constitutional right. The preliminary injunction is ordered stayed pending appeal.

Significance

It appears that while teachers have a constitutional right to *associate* for collective bargaining purposes, only a state statute can impose the *duty* to negotiate. Teachers' groups, therefore, may not enforce their desire to bargain with the board unless the duty is imposed upon the board by statute.

CASE CITATION: *Indianapolis Education Association v. Lewallen, et al., United States Court of Appeals, No. 17808, August 13, 1969*

32 Right of Teachers to Membership or Non-Membership in a Union

The factual situation revolved around the relationship of the MNEA and the board of education. The Wisconsin Employment Relations Board heard the complaints of the MNEA against the district and its superintendent, and held: 1) that in refusing and failing to renew a teacher's contract for the 1964–65 school year, the board discriminated against the teacher for the purpose of discouraging membership in and activities on behalf of the MNEA, and thus committed prohibited practices under the law; and 2) that by threatening its teachers with the forfeiture of two days' pay, if they failed to attend teachers' conventions and failed to retain membership in the sponsoring organization, interfered with, coerced, and restrained teachers in its employ of their right freely to affiliate with or decline to affiliate with, any employee organization, which is a prohibited practice under the Wisconsin statutes.

Relief Sought: Reversal of a judgment of the circuit court

Issue: Did the actions of the board constitute unfair labor practices as prohibited under the Wisconsin statutes?

Holding of the Trial Court: For the district

Holding of the Supreme Court of Wisconsin: Reversed

Reasoning

Teachers who do not wish to attend the teachers' convention cannot be required to do so under threat of loss of pay, but teachers who do not attend such conventions can be required to work for the school. In this way, teachers can avoid deductions from their salaries at the same time that they exercise their right to refuse to join an organization. If the teacher refuses to work, deductions from his salary could be made, but if the school does not offer work to teachers not attending conventions, the school cannot deny pay to such teachers. A board may not, under the Wisconsin law, terminate a teacher's contract because the teacher has been engaging in labor activities. Coercing teachers to join an employee organization is a prohibited practice under the law. The board discriminated against the teacher for the purpose of discouraging membership in and activities on behalf of the MNEA, and thereby committed a prohibited act. Quoting from a N.L.R.B. case (cited) "The issue before us is not, of course, whether or not there existed grounds for discharge of these employees apart from their union activity. *The fact that the employer had ample reason for discharging them is of no moment. It was free to discharge them for any reason good or bad, so long as it did not discharge them for their union activity.* And even though the discharges may have been based upon other reasons as well, if the employer were partly motivated by union activity, the discharges were violative of the Act." (Emphasis added.)

Significance

A court may review the evidence in an administrative body's hearings. Boards of education may not dismiss an employee because of his union activity alone. Teachers who do not wish to join an organization may not be made to do so, but the district must give them work if they choose not to attend the state teachers' convention.

CASE CITATION: *Muskego-Norway Consolidated Schools v. Wisconsin Employment Relations Board, 151 N.W.2d 617 (1967)*

AUTHOR'S COMMENTARY

In its full text of the decision, the Supreme Court of Wisconsin said in part:

> On the whole record we conclude that the WERB's finding No. 29 is supported by substantial evidence and reasonable inferences drawn therefrom in view of the entire record, that the failure to renew Koeller's teaching contract was motivated by his activities as chairman of the welfare committee of MNEA and not by any shortcomings Koeller may have had as a teacher nor upon his differences with certain policies of the school board and the respondent supervisory personnel.

One interesting aspect of this case was the issue of whether four administrators employed by the district were "agents" of the Muskego-Norway school board in order to impute their actions to the board in deciding whether unfair labor practices were committed. The trial court held that the actions of the supervisory personnel in question could not be attributed to the board in determining whether unfair labor practices had been committed, and only actions by school board members could be considered. The Wisconsin Supreme Court could not agree.

> The trial court's ruling places form over substance. Where the WERB expressly found that Kreuser, Refling, Ussel and Ladd were 'supervisory personnel in the employ of said School District,' such employment is sufficient to constitute an agency relationship. The employment policies of the school district are implemented through the actions of the supervisory personnel. Under the trial court's ruling, the school board could tacitly engage in unfair labor practices through actions by the supervisory personnel, and the employees discriminated against would have no effective recourse. Such a technical interpretation—as made by the trial court—of the findings of the WERB deprives the negotiations law of any real substance.

Finally, the teacher in question was given an opportunity to resign, but he refused. He was then handed a prepared notice of termination, the letter stating that the action was "deemed advisable in view of actions and conduct on your part which have previously been discussed with you."

Said the WERB in its analysis of the situation concerning the teacher:

> It seems incredible to us that the Superintendent could be sincere in the gravity of complaints made against Koeller and at the same time

offer to recommend him to another position. We believe this to be a gross act of intimidation. . . . In light of the entire record, we do not find that Koeller's competence as a teacher or disciplinarian motivated the determination not to extend his teaching contract.

33   *Organizational Activities of Teachers' Associations*

Contracts were not offered to three teachers who were officers of the local UBTA, after which the UBTA, with the assistance of the NJEA, posted "sanctions" against the Union Beach School District. Several thousand of these notices were sent to placement offices and other recipients advising them of the sanctions and encouraging teachers to stay away from the district. Thirty-one of the forty-seven teachers employed in the district submitted resignations to become effective two weeks before the end of the school term. The board then brought suit to enjoin the sanctions and to obtain a declaratory judgment outlining the legal status of "sanctions" against the district.

Relief Sought: Declaratory judgment that certain actions of the teachers' organization in invoking "sanctions" against the district were illegal

Issue: Do "sanctions" amount in effect to a strike and are they therefore illegal?

Holding of the Trial Court: For the plaintiff Board of Education

Holding of the Appellate Court: Affirmed

Reasoning

Employees of the board do not have the right to engage in collective bargaining. Defendants contend that no relief should be granted to plaintiff under the doctrine of clean hands. This, of course, assumes that there was misconduct on the part of plaintiff, which finding this court cannot make upon the evidence. . . . This court does not believe that unconstitutional conduct is justifiable . . . under any circumstances. . . . The stated purpose of the action taken by defendants was to make it impossible for the board to employ teachers in the school system. The fact that pressure was applied to persons in the teaching profession would of necessity cut down on the selection available to plaintiff. The board has in fact staffed its school for the 1967–68 school year; however, it must be remembered that defendants were restrained by a preliminary injunction. Pecuniary damages could not afford adequate compensation to plaintiff. Irreparable injury would be suffered by it if relief were not granted by this court. Because cases cited do not apply . . . and since the actions of defendants here have been found to be illegal, the cases are not in point.

Significance

Those who mount coercive efforts against the local board of education are not protected by the First Amendment right to freedom of speech. Teachers (with some exceptions) do not have collective bargaining rights unless given same by the state legislature. Sanctions amount in effect to a strike on the part of public school teachers, hence are illegal and injunction will lie to prevent their imposition by a teachers' organization against a school district.

CASE CITATION: *Board of Education, Borough of Union Beach v. New Jersey Education Association, 247 A.2d 867 (N.J. 1968)*

AUTHOR'S COMMENTARY

Because the UBTA and the NJEA had widely circulated notice of "sanctions" against the Union Beach School District, the court ordered the following means of squaring the account:

Defendants will be restrained and enjoined from making any press releases, notices or statements that "sanctions" have been or are being applied to plaintiff. UBTA, NJEA and NEA will be restrained and enjoined from in any way threatening censure, expulsion or any other action against any member of the teaching profession who accepts a position with plaintiff. Defendants NJEA and NEA will be required to give as wide distribution to the restraint as they gave to the "Notice of Professional Sanctions." The use of the word "sanctions" itself, applied for coercive purposes to plaintiff, a public agency, by UBTA, NJEA, and NEA, private associations, will be enjoined. There is no intention, however, of restraining defendants from exercising the right of free speech concerning what they think the conditions are in the Union Beach school system.

If the parties cannot agree on the form of a notice to be distributed and published, they may be heard at a mutually convenient time within the next two weeks.

The clean hands doctrine referred to in this case is an ethical concept long applied in the courts of equity in this country. It does not imply that the parties shall have led "blameless lives" but that they shall have acted without guilt or malice with respect to the issue then in litigation. Where, however, as in this case, defendants have engaged in an illegal practice, which the court said they did in engaging in "sanctions" against the plaintiff district, they could not then raise the clean hands doctrine on their own behalf.

As to the right of teachers' organizations to strike, the courts have almost uniformly held that injunctive relief will lie to block such a move on the part of public school teachers' organizations. For example, in *School District for the City of Holland, v. Holland Education Association,* 157 N.W.2d 206 (Mich. 1967), the court found that a concerted failure to report for duty and willful absence from the full, faithful and proper performance of their duties of employment for the purpose of inducing, influencing, or coercing a change in their working conditions amounted in effect to a strike, and was therefore amenable to injunctive relief.

The majority opinion, however, concluded that teachers could not be enjoined from striking simply because of the "impact" on children where schools were not in session. Although the courts have the power to grant injunctive relief, the Michigan statute does not compel them to do so in every instance in which public employees strike. The opinion seems to say that there may be instances in which public employees might be allowed to express their dissatisfaction with working conditions or their relationships with government boards and the courts would not interfere with the right to do so by issuing temporary injunctive relief.

Similarly, where teachers called in sick, the Commissioner of Education for the State of New Jersey held that the board was not acting unreasonably when it required those who were absent on the two days in question to furnish doctor's certificates in order to draw their salaries for those two days. The Camden school district had 883 teachers in its school system. Over the years the number of teachers absent from their employment because of illness or other sick leave causes on any one day averaged approximately 50. On January 4, 1967, 446 teachers called the school office to report that they would not be at work on account of illness. On January 5, 368 called to make a like report. As a result of the mass absenteeism, the school board obtained an injunction restraining the Camden Education Association and the American Federation of Teachers and their members from absenting themselves or impeding the operation of the Camden school system.

Wilma Farmer and others who had been required to file a physician's certificate in order to collect their pay for the two days brought an action before the Commissioner of Education, *Wilma Farmer v. Board of Education of the City of Camden,* Commissioner of Education Opinion No. LXXII, October 10, 1967. The official found that the board was within its rights in requiring teachers to furnish sufficient proof, and where proof was lacking to refuse to pay the teachers for those days in question. Absenting themselves on a "mass sickness" basis amounted in effect to a strike, which was prohibited in New Jersey.

In Pennsylvania, a taxpayer, angered at the fact that the school board had rewarded teachers for striking by increasing their salaries, brought suit to enjoin the payment of the increase as a violation of the state's "Strike by Public Employees Act." In *Legman v. School District,* 247 A.2d 566, Pa. 1969 the court dismissed a complaint with the reasoning that unless a taxpayer brings a suit in equity, there would be no way to require a board of education to live up to the terms of the no-strike act.

The first "state-wide" strike of teachers occurred in the State of Florida. The Supreme Court of that state declared that a strike by public school teachers could be enjoined. *Pinellas County Classroom Teachers' Association v. Board of Public Instruction,* 214 So.2d 34, Fla. 1969. In the dispute, the board had obtained a temporary injunction to prohibit the teachers from failing to come to work. The teachers' association claimed that their refusal to go to work until certain items pertaining to working conditions could be agreed upon and placed in the contract did not amount to a strike within the meaning of the state's anti-strike law for public employees. The court said that the teachers were attempting to bring pressure upon the school board by refusing to go to work, but at the same time they laid claim to their positions and asserted the right to go back to work on terms more acceptable to them. "This, indeed," said the court, "was a typical strike."

The Indiana Supreme Court narrowly upheld by a vote of 3–2 the concept that "the overwhelming weight of authority in the United States is that government employees may not engage in a strike for any purpose." Some teachers in the City of Anderson went on strike and the board obtained a temporary restraining order. This led to the court's finding that the Local 519, Anderson Federation of Teachers was in contempt of court for violating the restraining order. The Indiana Supreme Court held that the trial court "was in all things correct in its finding and judgment of contempt of court." *Anderson Federation of Teachers, Local 519 v. School City of Anderson,* Indiana Supreme Court, October 1, 1969. The case is interesting for the minority opinion written by Justice C. J. DeBruler, who argued that the strike was entirely peaceful and minimally disruptive of the public service rendered by the school. "It is naïve to think that every strike by any public employees will upset the whole operation of government," wrote DeBruler.

The minority opinion continued:

> Indiana needs a comprehensive labor relations act which would provide a mechanism to help settle labor disputes involving both public and private employees, without recourse to a strike. It is obvious the courts cannot create this machinery. It is equally obvious that the Court should not create an apparent substitute in the form of a *per se* rule

against peaceful strikes by public employees regardless of the impact of the strike. I believe that until the Legislature acts further, the Court should apply the anti-injunction act in cases of strikes by public employees and not a judicial version of martial law. To prohibit a strike in a context where this amounts to ending any pressure on the employer to bargain in good faith with representatives of the employees may do long lasting damage to the community.

Acting from this limited minority position—that collective bargaining for public employees will remain incomplete until the strike is legalized—the states in 1971 were just beginning to experiment cautiously with this concept. However, the courts were continuing as before to refuse to permit the strike by teachers in the absence of statutory authority.

34 *Constitutionality of Collective Bargaining Legislation for Teachers*

The Washington statute governing employee negotiations required school boards to negotiate with teacher organizations which had won an employee election and granted boards the authority to adopt rules and regulations for the administration of employer-employee relations. The American Federation of Teachers, Yakima Local 1485, brought suit against the board to enjoin the counting of ballots on the ground that the statute was unconstitutional. The contention was that 1) there were no procedures for conducting an election, and 2) the title of the act mentioned nothing about representative elections for employees and therefore the statute was invalid because its subject was not fairly expressed in its title.

> *Relief Sought:* Injunction against board election to determine employee representation agent

> *Issue:* Is a statute authorizing school districts to adopt reasonable rules and regulations for the administration of employer-employee relations unconstitutional?

> *Holding of the Trial Court:* For the board

> *Holding of the Supreme Court of Washington:* Affirmed

Reasoning

School districts are municipal or quasi-municipal corporations created by the state. The legislature may confer powers of local regulation, or administrative powers, on municipal corporations without violating the constitutional prohibition of improper delegation of legislative power. Here the giving of the power to hold an election to the local board by the legislature was an exercise of its discretion, so long as there are detailed standards and guidelines furnished, and so long as those powers relate to local purposes of regulation or administration. . . . The court dismissed the second contention of the union by saying that ". . . the title of an act need not be an index of its contents. It suffices if the title embraces, and reasonably gives notice of, the contents of the act."

Significance

Apparently, the delegation of some discretionary authority to local school boards to hold elections and to use its own methods of carrying out the intent of a legislative act is not unconstitutional so long as there are guidelines and standards sufficiently clear to guide the local board in the exercise of its duty.

CASE CITATION: *American Federation of Teachers v. Yakima School District, 447 P.2d 593 (Wash. 1968)*

AUTHOR'S COMMENTARY

In *San Francisco Classroom Teachers Association v. Board of Education,* Superior Court Judgment No. 588011, August 26, 1968, the court upheld the constitutionality of the Winton Act, which required the board and superintendent to meet and confer in good faith with representatives of the certificated employees organizations, and attempt to reach an agreement with them. The association had claimed that the act precluded representatives of rival organizations from presenting proposals directly to the board because of the provision in the act for a Negotiating Council. The court could not agree, and said that the board would henceforth be enjoined permanently from "meeting and conferring or signing agreements directly with representatives of the defendant Federation or any other certificated employee organization with regard to matters set forth in Section 13084 and 13085 of the Education code, outside of and without regard to the Negotiating Council. . . ."

The court also issued an order to the board in question to "meet and confer in good faith and endeavor to reach agreements with representatives of certificated employee organizations, including representatives of the defendant Federation, only through the Negotiating Council" as set forth in the Winton Act. The act provided for "proportional representation" of both organizations on the Negotiating Council, such representation being pro-rated as to the strength of each organization in the particular district in question. It was this latter feature of the act which was claimed to make the act unconstitutional, among other things. But in its terse statement of judgment, the court said that the legislature meant in effect what it had said in the act, and its intent was not to be avoided through a declaration that the act was unconstitutional.

35   *Congressional Control of Education*

The State of Maryland, and 27 other states and one school district joined, sought to enjoin enforcement of the Fair Labor Standards amendments of 1966 as unconstitutional excess of congressional power under the commerce clause. A three-judge United States District Court, 269 F.Supp. 826, determined that such an application (of the "enterprise concept") was not unconstitutional, and plaintiffs appealed to the United States Supreme Court, which affirmed the holding of the court below.

Relief Sought: Declaration that the 1966 minimum wage amendments to the Fair Labor Standards Act, insofar as they applied to employees of states, were unconstitutional

Issue: Was the extension of the "enterprise concept" to cover state institutions an over-reach of the power of the Congress?

Holding of the U. S. District Court: For defendant

Holding of the United States Supreme Court: Affirmed

Reasoning

The term "enterprise engaged in commerce or in the production of goods for commerce" is defined by 29 U.S.C. § 203 to mean "an enterprise which has employees engaged in commerce or in the production of goods for commerce, including employees handling, selling or otherwise working on goods that have been moved in or produced for commerce by any person. . . ." Maryland is a substantial user of goods imported from other states: 87% of the $8 million spent for supplies and equipment by its public school system during the fiscal year 1965 represented direct interstate purchases. Strikes and work stoppages involving employees of schools and hospitals, events which unfortunately are not infrequent, obviously interrupt and burden this flow of goods across state lines. It is therefore clear that a "rational basis" exists for congressional standards for schools and hospitals, as for other importing enterprises. This Court has ample power to prevent what the appellants purport to fear, "the utter destruction of the State as a sovereign political entity." In dissenting, Justices Douglas and Stewart wrote that "the National Government may not 'interfere unduly with the State's performance of its sovereign functions of government. . . . In this case the State as a sovereign power is being seriously tampered with, potentially crippled'."

Significance

The minimum wage amendments to the Fair Labor Standards Act were extended to cover, *inter alia,* nonprofessional, nonexecutive, and nonadministrative employees of state public schools, hospitals, and related institutions and such an extension of the coverage is not unconstitutional.

CASE CITATION: *Maryland v. Wirtz, Secretary of Labor, 88 S.Ct. 2017 (Md. 1968)*

36 First Amendment Rights of Teachers to Join Unions

An action for damages was brought against the superintendent and the elected members of a board of education by two probationary teachers, one of whom was not re-employed and the other of whom was dismissed before the end of the second year of teaching. Reasons for these actions were that the teachers were engaged in distributing union materials and soliciting union membership, it was alleged. Each sought $100,000 damages. The court below dismissed the suit on the grounds that the teachers had no First Amendment right to form or join a labor union. The Court of Appeals, however, held that a complaint alleging that a non-tenure teacher was dismissed solely because of his membership in a union states a claim upon which relief can be granted under the Civil Rights Act of 1871. The case was reversed and remanded for trial.

Relief Sought: Damages under the Civil Rights Act of 1871 against the superintendent and the elected members of a board of education

Issue: Does union activity leading to dismissal of a teacher state a claim upon which relief can be granted under the Civil Rights Act of 1871?

Holding of the Federal District Court: Dismissed

Holding of the Court of Appeals: Reversed and remanded for trial

Reasoning

The superintendent and the elected members of the board of education were not absolutely immune from suit for alleged discrimination in dismissing teachers for their union membership. The court held that the First Amendment confers the right to form and join a labor union. Under this amendment, public school teachers have a right of free association. Any undue interference with this right violates the due process clause of the Fourteenth Amendment. Public employment may not be subjected to unreasonable conditions; where public school teachers assert their First Amendment rights it will not usually warrant their dismissal. There is a remedy for being deprived of their rights, however: the Civil Rights Act of 1871. Nor were the officials protected under the Illinois Tort Immunity Act; under the supremacy clause, this statute must give way to a federal statute. Even if the union was engaged in unlawful activities, the two teachers, as members, could not be held to account for their organization's misdeeds. Section 1983 of Title 42 of the U.S. Code provides: "Every person who, under color of any statute, ordinance, regulation, custom, or usage, of any State or Territory, subjects, or causes to be subjected, any citizen of the United States or other person within the jurisdiction thereof to the deprivation of any rights, privileges, or immunities secured by the Constitution and laws, shall be liable to the party injured in an action at law, suit in equity, or other proper proceeding for redress."

Significance

School board members and school superintendents should avoid discriminating against an employee of the district in the exercise of his constitutional rights. To do so may subject them to a suit for damages grounded on the Civil Rights Act of 1871 and the due process clause of the Fourteenth Amendment.

CASE CITATION: *McLaughlin v. Tilendis, 398 F.2d 287 (Ill. 1968)*

AUTHOR'S COMMENTARY

Ordinarily, elected school board members acting in good faith and within the scope of their powers cannot be held personally liable for their torts even though such actions may increase the amount of the district's indebtedness or work a hardship on third parties. A new dimension has been added to school board members' personal liability, however, with the introduction of the concept that it is an invasion of a third party's constitutional rights to discriminate against him because of his membership in a union, or because of his or her sex, or because he exercises his constitutional right to free speech and/or assembly. The pertinent statute is that invoked in *McLaughlin v. Tilendis,* 398 F.2d 287 (Ill. 1968), in which the Court of Appeals for the Seventh Circuit held that a complaint alleging that a non-tenure teacher was dismissed solely because of his membership in a union states a claim upon which relief can be granted under the Civil Rights Act of 1871.

Section 1983 of Title 42 of the U.S. Code provides: "Every person, who, under color of any statute, ordinance, regulation, custom, or usage, of any State or Territory, subjects, or causes to be subjected, any citizen of the United States or other person within the jurisdiction thereof to the deprivation of any rights, privileges, or immunities secured by the Constitution and laws, shall be liable to the party injured in an action at law, suit in equity, or other proper proceeding for redress." (17 stat. 13, 1871.)

Such cases are tried to the federal courts on the grounds of deprivation of due process under the Fourteenth Amendment and/or a violation of the Civil Rights Act of 1871, and present a problem for the superintendent and elected board members whose insurance does not cover such exigencies. There appears, therefore, to be a need for sufficient insurance coverage to render harmless these public officials in the exercise of their duties, where, either intentionally or inadvertently, they transgress the conditions of the act in question, or otherwise deprive a person of his rights under the Constitution.

Nearly every state has its anti-discrimination act, and Illinois (where *Tilendis* originated) had its Illinois Tort Immunity Act, but under the supremacy clause, federal legislation takes precedence over such state legislation. Ordinarily, the question of discriminatory activities on the part of a board of education would find relief under the state's anti-discrimination act, where the relief would amount to a cease-and-desist order against the board. But the *Tilendis* case has opened the door for the courts to consider the whole broad sweep of constitutional law and its applicability to public employees, chiefly teachers.

There should be some protection for public officials who serve unselfishly in the capacity of boards of education members, but who through no apparent fault of their own, have run afoul of the law on an allegation that they have invaded an employee's constitutional rights. While the indications are that the incidence of such litigation would not be high, it will no doubt increase, and where it will strike none can tell.

Another case involving the applicability of the Civil Rights Act of 1871 to public employment came before the Court of Appeals of the Eighth Circuit on January 17, 1969. The principal question raised was whether governmental employees, here two street department employees of the City of North Platte, Nebraska, discharged because they had joined a labor union, had a right to action for damages and injunctive relief under the Act. The court held that they did possess such a right.

The City argued that the plaintiffs had no federally protected right to be continued in their employment. In overriding their argument, the court quoted from *In re Summers,* 325 U.S. 561 (1945) at 571, in which the United States Supreme Court had said:

We need not pause to consider whether an abstract right to public employment exists. It is sufficient to say that constitutional protection does extend to the public servant whose exclusion . . . is patently arbitrary or discriminatory.

"No paramount public interest of the State of Nebraska or the City of North Platte warranted limiting the plaintiffs' right to freedom of association. To the contrary, it is the public policy of Nebraska that employment should not be denied on the basis of union membership. The Constitution of the State and the various laws (citing) specifically provide that 'no person shall be denied employment because of membership in or affiliation with . . . a labor organization.' " *American Federation of State, County, and Municipal Employees, AFL-CIO v. Milton Woodward,* 406 F.2d 137, Nebr. 1969.

PART THREE

Cases Related to
Student Unrest,
Dismissal, and Discipline

Part Three

Cases Related to Student Unrest, Dismissal, and Discipline

*F*or the first time in our nation's history, the United States Supreme Court in 1969 entertained a case involving student discipline and control not having religious overtones. (See *Tinker v. Des Moines Independent Community School District*, 89 S.Ct. 733, Iowa 1969, Case No. 21 for a brief of this case.) The Court held that, in the absence of disruption of the school program, high school students have the right to wear black armbands in school as a means of protesting against the war in Viet Nam. "Our Constitution," said the Court, "says that we must take this risk"—that of deviations from the majority opinion. Such a right is protected under the First Amendment and cannot be prohibited without evidence that "it materially and substantially interferes with the requirements of appropriate discipline in the operation of the school." This section is concerned with the rise of student unrest in this country, and in the cases which have come before the court on the discipline and control of such students by boards of education, school administrators, and teachers.

In refusing to accept the case on certiorari, the United States Supreme Court on June 1, 1970 in effect upheld a district court ruling against a dress code in a Wisconsin school district. *Breen v. Kahl*, 296 F.Supp. 702, Wisc. 1969, Case No. 46. There the board contended that the following regulation was valid:

> Hair should be washed, combed and worn so it does not hang below the collar line in the back, over the ears on the side and must be above the eyebrows. Boys should be clean shaven; long sideburns are out.

The court below said that the freedom enjoyed by an adult to present himself or herself to the world in the manner of his or her choice is a "highly protected freedom," and any effort by the state to impair or limit this right must bear "a substantial burden of justification."

In colonial days, parents were fully responsible for the upbringing and education of their children, but as the state gradually took over this responsibility, there arose a need for an adult to supervise and "stand in" for the parent. This legal fiction became known in this country by its Latin derivative *in loco parentis*, "in place of the parent." The teacher became charged with a parent's rights, duties, and responsibilities, and the norm became that behavior or standard of care which the reasonable parent would provide under the same or similar circumstances. Thus, one of the prerogatives of every teacher and administrator is that of disciplining and directing the work and the upbringing of the child under his care and supervision. Of course, the control over the student by the teacher or administrator must at all times stand the test of reasonableness. The rule must be reasonable, and its application must likewise be reasonable to the time and place involved. For example, in *Pugsley v. Sellmeyer*, 250 S.W. 538, Ark. 1923, the court upheld a board ruling that the use of plain talcum powder on a girl's face was prohibited in school. Such a ruling would no doubt be unreasonable today.

Although their children are by law required to attend school, parents still retain considerable control over them, sharing their control with the teacher and administrator. Three areas are still the province of the parent: 1) control of what religious instruction, if any, the child shall receive; 2) control of the extent to which he shall be medically treated if at all; and 3) control over the inner recesses of his mind and the right to guard against any invasion thereof. Thus, the parent still retains control of the child's soul, body and mind even though he has in effect turned his child over to the state for educational purposes. It is this area—that of instruction—which is the special province of the teacher, and the area in which his control over the child is legally strongest.

37   *Parental Control over the Student*

Plaintiff's son was suspended from school for wearing metal heel plates on his shoes following the adoption of a rule by the board against any boy wearing such plates to school. Plaintiff insisted that the regulation in question was unreasonable and that he had the right to order his son to wear metal heel plates despite the rule. Defendant school board claimed that the hardwood floors of the school were being damaged by the plates and that the metal heel plates also caused extreme noise and disorder in and around the building which interfered with the discipline, government, and instruction of the pupils in attendance. The trial court upheld the board's rule, and the plaintiff appealed to a higher court.

Relief Sought: Restraint against enforcement of a rule prohibiting students from wearing metal heel plates to school

Issue: Does a public school board have the right to expel a student for insubordination when the student disobeys a school rule under the direction of his parents?

Holding of the Trial Court: For the board of education

Holding of the Appellate Court: Affirmed

Reasoning

The rule of the defendant school board was clearly reasonable since it was based on conserving school property and maintaining good order and discipline. Although the plaintiff's son was an excellent student and was not indolent or disorderly, his action of obeying his parents' command in wearing the heel plates constituted insubordination for which he could be legally suspended and later expelled. No reasonable school rule or regulation can be enforced by the school if parents are allowed to instruct the pupil to ignore it. The members of the board acted wholly and entirely in good faith. As a general rule, the decision of a school board if exercised in good faith is final insofar as relates to the right of pupils to enjoy school privileges and the courts will not interfere with the exercise of such authority unless it has been illegally or unreasonably exercised.

Significance

The rules necessary to proper conduct and management of the schools are and of necessity ought to be left to the discretion of the local board, whose acts will not be set aside by the courts unless there is clear abuse of the power conferred.

CASE CITATION: *Stromberg v. French, 236 N.W. 477 (N. D. 1931)*

38   *Control of Married Students*

A father on behalf of his son sought to restrain enforcement of a board resolution which prohibited married students or previously married students from participating in any school activities except classroom work. Such students were prohibited from participating in athletics and could not hold class office or other positions of honor. Academic honors such as Valedictorian and Salutatorian were exceptions. Young Kissick was married in March, 1959 after having attended the Garland school and having earned an athletic letter in football. Both Kissick and his wife were underage. The school board resolution was passed in August, 1959 and was retroactive. The resolution was attacked as being unreasonable, discriminatory, and unconstitutional, and in violation of public policy in that it penalized marriage, that it violated the Fourteenth Amendment of the Constitution of the United States, and that the resolution did not apply to young Kissick since it was passed after the marriage.

Relief Sought: Injunction to restrain enforcement of a board resolution

Issue: May a school board prohibit married high school students from participating in parts of the public school activities program other than classroom work?

Holding of the Trial Court: For the defendant School Board

Holding of the Appellate Court: Affirmed

Reasoning

With regard to the authority of school trustees, it is generally held that the courts will interfere in such matters only where a clear abuse of power and discrimination are made to appear. The court looks with favor upon marriage; however, public policy is unfavorable toward "underage" marriage. The Texas Constitution states: "A statute cannot be said to be retroactive law prohibited by the Constitution unless it can be shown that the application of the law would take away or impair vested rights acquired under existing law." But young Kissick did not have vested rights to play football, but merely had a contingent or expected right to do so. Other than this, he had full constitutional rights to pursue his academic endeavors. Due to the fact that the school board passed the resolution in question with the objective of discouraging "teen-age" marriages, the court could not find the resolution to be arbitrary, unreasonable, discriminatory, or capricious, nor did it deprive the plaintiff's son of his constitutional rights.

Significance

While it is doubtful that a student could be expelled from school for marriage, it is well settled law that his activities may be limited to those involving classroom work only. A board resolution passed after the marriage and applied retroactively does not deprive the student of his constitutional rights unless he has acquired some vested right to engage in the activity in question.

CASE CITATION: *Kissick v. Garland Independent School District, 330 S.W.2d 708 (Texas 1959)*

AUTHOR'S COMMENTARY

The incidence of student marriages and the subsequent litigation involving this phenomenon are on the increase. However, the courts are in agreement that 1) the student may not be deprived of his right to attend school upon the basis of his or her marriage alone and 2) the student's right to participate in extra-curricular activities may legally be limited. One could justifiably reason that if anyone needs an education, it is the underage married student. Therefore, to limit his right to obtain an education apparently is seen as a denial of the right to equal educational opportunity.

This philosophy of law was well stated in *Starkey v. Board of Education of David County School District*, 381 P.2d 718, Utah 1963, with these words:

> An individual has a constitutional right both to attend school and get married, but he has no "right" to compel the board of education to allow him to participate in school extra-curricular activities when the board has decreed marriage to be a bar to participation therein. Participation in extra-curricular school activities is a privilege which may be claimed only in accordance with standards set up for participation therein.

Most of the judges have said that it is not for them to be concerned with the wisdom or propriety of the resolution or its social desirability, nor whether it best serves the objectives of education, nor with whether it is convenient or inconvenient in its application to the plaintiff. So long as the resolution is deemed by the board of education to serve the purpose of best promoting the objectives of the school and the standards for eligibility are based on uniformly applied classifications which bear some reasonable relationship to the objectives, it cannot be said to be capricious, arbitrary, or unjustly discriminatory.

It appears, however, that marriage may free a female student who is underage from the compulsory school attendance requirement. In *In re State in the Interest of Goodwin*, 39 So. 2d 731, La. 1949, a girl of fourteen while at home ill phoned her principal and informed him that she was going to get married. When she did not report for school the following day, the principal charged her with truancy. After a preliminary hearing, she was held as a juvenile delinquent pending further hearing. While under the court's jurisdiction, she was released for a short time on Sunday and during this release she was married. Following the marriage, she returned to the detention home. She brought suit claiming that her marriage "emancipated" her. The court in upholding her claim noted that a married woman is not a child under parental control and is not subject to the compulsory attendance laws which may obtain in that particular state.

Some of the cases are tied up in litigation until after the student has graduated. In *Board of Education of Independent School District of Waterloo v. Green,* 147 N.W.2d 854, Iowa 1967, plaintiff claimed that the case was moot because he had finished his high school requirements by that time. But the court said it would rule on the case nonetheless because it "was a case which would likely recur," and other school boards would need a precedent on which to act. It then held that while plaintiff had a right both to attend school and to marry, he had no right to compel the board to exercise its discretion to his personal advantage so he could participate in basketball activities.

A Tennessee case appears to be unique in that the court allowed temporary exclusion from school because of student marriage. The court found that, on the basis of sworn experts in the field (the high school principals), the board had undertaken the rule in question. But it was emphasized that the rule was to apply on a temporary basis, and was not so severe as to permanently exclude the married pupils from the school.

The case is cited as *State v. Marion County Board of Education,* 302 S.W.2d 57, Tenn. 1957.

In *State v. Chamberlain,* 175 N.E.2d 539, Ohio 1962, a school board asked a married pregnant student to withdraw from school. The board rule was to the effect that the student was to withdraw after discovery of the pregnancy. Homebound instruction was provided and the board emphasized that its concern was for the protection of the girl and was not punitive in nature. Under these circumstances, the court upheld the rule.

39 *Corporal Punishment*

Suits brought this action against the teacher Glover for an alleged assault and battery upon his eight year old son. Evidence was conflicting on two points at the trial: 1) the type of instrument used to administer the punishment, and 2) the severity of the punishment. The father claimed his son was chastised with a slat from an apple crate while the teacher said he used a ping pong paddle, commonly used in that school for administration of such punishment. The parent claimed the punishment was excessive; the teacher said that he paddled the boy on the buttocks only, the skin was not broken, and five licks were administered.

A medical expert testified that there was no permanent damage to the child. The evidence tended to show that there had been an infraction of the school rules by the boy, and further that the teacher was in no wise angry or aggravated with the boy when the spanking took place. Mr. Glover was responsible for maintaining order and discipline in the school.

Relief Sought: Damages for alleged assault and battery

Issue: When do corporal punishment rights of the teacher become assault and battery for which recovery in damages may be had?

Holding of the Trial Court: For defendant teacher

Holding of the Appellate Court: Judgment affirmed

Reasoning

A teacher is regarded as standing *in loco parentis* to those under his care and keeping and has authority to administer moderate correction to pupils under his care. To be guilty of assault and battery a school teacher must administer punishment that is immoderate and do so with legal malice considering 1) the instrument used, 2) nature of the offense, 3) age of the child, 4) condition of the child's health, and 5) other attendant circumstances, such as whether there was permanent injury as a result of the chastisement. The weight of the evidence present did not support the father's claim that the punishment was immoderate or that the teacher acted in a malicious way in administering the punishment.

Significance

To be held liable for assault and battery on a pupil, the teacher must administer immoderate punishment considering the circumstances, or must act from legal malice or wicked motives. If these are absent, the teacher has the right, standing *in loco parentis,* to administer moderate punishment considering the instrument used, the age, size, strength and health of the child, the nature of the offense, and other circumstantial elements. The norm is that standard of care which the normal parent would use in the same or similar circumstances, which is ordinarily a question of fact for the jury.

CASE CITATION: *Suits v. Glover, 71 So.2d 49 (Ala. 1954)*

AUTHOR'S COMMENTARY

Apparently, a teacher does not exceed his authority by punishing a child even though the act complained of occurred outside school hours and off school property. The leading case on this point is *Lander v. Seaver,* 32 Vt.

114, 1859. A father sent his son after the family cow, and on the way, while driving the cow past the schoolmaster's home, the boy made a disparaging remark against the schoolmaster and before other students. The next day at school the schoolmaster whipped the boy, whereupon the father brought suit for damages, saying that the schoolmaster had exceeded his authority.

The court could not agree with the contention of the father. Since the offense had a direct and immediate intent to injure the school and undermine the schoolmaster's authority in the presence of other students, the court held that the teacher was acting within his rights in punishing the boy when he did again return to school.

In *Andreozzi v. Rubano,* 141 A.2d 639, Conn. 1958, the question before the court was whether a teacher who violated a school rule against personally punishing a boy for insubordination could be held to account for assault and battery. A boy of fifteen, unruly and creating a disturbance, was in the school's detention room. The teacher, intending to lead the boy from the room, took him by the arm, but he pulled away and became loud and profane. The teacher accompanied the boy from the room in order to talk privately with him in the hall. Away from the other pupils, the boy clenched his fists, assumed a belligerent attitude, and uttered a vulgar remark to the teacher. Believing that the boy intended to strike him, the teacher slapped him across the face with the back of his hand.

The school district had a written policy that corporal punishment could be inflicted only by the principal of the school in the presence of the teacher. Evidence respecting the character and past conduct of the pupil in the school was introduced.

The court held that, despite the school rule to the contrary, the teacher had acted within his rights in disciplining the unruly pupil. He had acted, not for the purpose of inflicting punishment, but to restore order and discipline. If he had not taken an action in the face of the boy's sudden and violent outburst, he would have lost face before the other pupils; the order and discipline of the school would have been seriously affected. There may also have been some evidence that the teacher acted in self-defense, although this was not taken up by the court in reaching its decision.

In *People v. Baldini,* 159 N.Y.S.2d 802, 1957 the court in upholding the teacher's right to discipline the pupil, said in part: "The teacher must be supreme in his classroom. The legislature has cloaked the teacher with authority so that he may maintain the authority and decorum necessary for the proper conduct of the classroom. There was no malice on the part of the defendant (teacher) and in light of the pupil's conduct, the actions of the teacher (here) were not such that would warrant a conviction of assault in the third degree."

40   *Corporal Punishment*

Plaintiff was a boy of ten, small for his age, weighing 89 pounds. Defendant was the principal, a man of 46, weighing 190 pounds. The boy's teacher, in attempting to punish him for disobedience, was resisted by the boy in her attempts to strike his hands with a strap. The principal happened by chance to be passing the room, and was called in to witness another unsuccessful attempt at punishment. The teacher then handed the strap to the principal. The principal ordered the boy to go to his office, but the boy refused to move. The principal then pulled the boy from the room by grasping the boy's wrist. A struggle ensued. The principal pushed the boy to the floor, kneeling on the boy's abdomen with one knee. The boy struggled to get free from under the principal's weight. The boy's sister was called, and she was instructed to take the boy home. In the struggle the boy sustained a skin burn or abrasion causing a break in the skin from which osteomyelitis resulted.

Relief Sought: Damages for personal injuries in school

Issue: When do acts on the part of the teacher amount to undue or excessive punishment or restraint for which damages will lie?

Holding of the Trial Court: For the plaintiff

Holding of the Appellate Court: Affirmed

Reasoning

It is well settled that the teacher or principal may require obedience to reasonable rules and may inflict reasonable corporal punishment. No precise rule for excessive or unreasonable punishment exists. Each case must be considered on its own merits. The trial court found from the facts that it might logically be inferred that the weight of the defendant was exerted upon the plaintiff, and that the privilege or indulgence in the exercise of defendant's discretion terminated and that there was an excess of restraint imposed when plaintiff sought to escape the crushing weight of the defendant. There is no difference between acts of restraint and corporal punishment. The restraint here was unreasonable and the plaintiff was justified in attempting to escape the crushing weight.

Significance

Although the teacher or principal has a legal right to restrain or punish a child under his care and supervision, this right is not without limit. Each case must rest upon its own merits as to when reasonable, hence permissible restraint or punishment ends, and unreasonable, or prohibitory restraint or punishment begins.

CASE CITATION: *Calway v. Williamson, 35 A.2d 377 (Conn. 1944)*

AUTHOR'S COMMENTARY

Assault and battery may be either a civil or a criminal action, depending upon the complaint. In a civil action, the relief sought is damages, while in a criminal action, the state is the plaintiff and the relief sought is prosecution for breaking a law.

In most instances, civil action is brought against the teacher to recover damages. Where the teacher carries liability insurance, the insuror must pick up the tab when a finding of assault and battery makes the teacher liable to the student.

A considerable number of cases in which teachers and/or administrators have been held liable for damages have come before the courts. In general, the following rules apply to avoid such litigation, or to escape liability:

1. Make sure that the rule is a reasonable one, and that the punishment is fitted to the crime. Where, for example, the teacher hit a boy "pretty hard" because he would not speak up loudly enough to be heard, the teacher was held liable.

2. Be sure that the rule is reasonably administered, that it applies equally to all students, and that it is not arbitrary or capricious in its administration. One could have a reasonable rule, but administer it in such a way that it would be unreasonable.

3. Fit the punishment to the age, size, sex, physical condition and general ability of the student; to exceed in any of these elements may amount to cruel and inhuman treatment.

4. Always use the place that nature intended when administering corporal punishment. A teacher had to pay in damages when he hit the child on the side of the head, and a broken ear drum resulted.

5. Finally, avoid any show of anger, vindictiveness, or viciousness in administering corporal punishment. The act of administering punishment when in the heat of anger or to get even with the child is not permitted. Remember, the purpose of punishment is for the benefit of the child, and to keep order in the school, not to vindicate the teacher's rule. Thus, corporal punishment should be administered in the same manner and mode

as a reasonable parent would administer it under the same or similar circumstances.

41   Search of the Student

Billy Marlar, a boy between ten and eleven years of age, attended public school in Memphis. The boy violated a school rule by going into the classroom during recess. When confronted by the teacher, he denied this, but later confessed when witnesses were produced (two other pupils who had seen him). The teacher reproached the boy, and turned him over to the superintendent, Miss Bill, for punishment. The superintendent inflicted slight punishment with a ruler. A dime was discovered to be missing from the room which the boy had entered. The boy's pockets were searched, not so much to find the missing dime, as to vindicate the boy from charge or suspicion which rested upon him at the time because of his having committed the other offense and falsified about it. Action was brought by the boy through his friend against the superintendent and the teacher for assault and battery and illegal search.

Relief Sought: Damages for assault and battery and search of person

Issue: May a teacher be held liable under the circumstances for assault and battery and for illegal search?

Holding of the Trial Court: Case dismissed

Holding of Circuit Court and Court of Appeals: Dismissed

Holding of the Supreme Court: Affirmed

Reasoning

All authorities seem to agree on the general principle that the teacher stands in the stead, in a somewhat limited sense, of the parent, and may exercise such powers of control and correction, including physical punishment, as may be reasonably necessary. There must be a lack of malice, a reasonable ground for the punishment, and the punishment must be commensurate with the offense. The courts below reasoned that the punishment was indeed reasonable and that it suited the offense. With regard to the search of the plaintiff's person the court said, "The proof indicates a primary purpose (of the search) was to clear (the boy's) honor from suspicion (of stealing the dime) and thus benefit the pupil." Both the superintendent and the teacher were experienced and had excellent reputations. They acted as a reasonably prudent parent would have acted under the same or similar circumstances and their actions should not be set aside under these circumstances.

Significance

If the search is for the purpose of vindicating the pupil's honor and not for punitive purposes, it appears that a search of his person is not illegal.

CASE CITATION: *Marlar v. Bill, 178 S.W.2d 634 (Tenn. 1944)*

42   Search of the Student's Locker

Defendant was a high school student. On the day after a local music store was robbed, two policemen came to the school and talked with the defendant about the robbery. The high school principal, on request of the officers, with the consent of the defendant, and upon his own judgment, opened the boy's locker. A key was found which later led to the discovery in a bus depot of a cache of goods stolen from the music store, among which were some easily identifiable coins. Defendant was convicted and he appealed, alleging among other things that no "Miranda" warning had been provided him, and that the evidence obtained during the search of his school locker was illegally obtained, that he had a right to remain silent, and not give his consent to the search, and that he had a right to be represented by counsel at all times in the proceedings. The Supreme Court of Kansas upheld the search on the grounds that the "Miranda" warning did not apply to search and seizure situations involving a school locker.

Issue: May school officials search a student's locker?

Holding of the Trial Court: Convicted defendant of robbery

Holding of the Kansas Supreme Court: Affirmed

Reasoning

Although a student may have control of his school locker as against fellow students, his possession is not exclusive against the school and its officials. A school does not supply it students with lockers for illicit use in harboring pilfered property or harmful substances. We deem it a proper function of school authorities to inspect the lockers under their control and to prevent their use in illicit ways or for illegal purposes. We believe this right of inspection is inherent in the authority vested in school administrators and that the same must be retained and exercised in the management of our schools if their educational functions are to be maintained and the welfare of the student bodies preserved. The court quoted with approval a New York case in which it was decided that school officials have not only the right to inspect student lockers but also the duty to do so when suspicion arises that something of an illicit nature may be secreted there.

Significance

While the student has privacy against other students in his school locker, he does not have exclusive privacy against school officials, who, acting in their managerial capacity, cooperate with the law enforcement officials. The question of student lockers, and their search, however, is not fully settled as a matter of law.

    CASE CITATION: *State v. Stein, 456 P.2d 1 (Kans. 1969)*

AUTHOR'S COMMENTARY

The Fourth Amendment guarantees the right of citizens to be secure in their persons, houses, papers, and effects against *unreasonable* searches and seizures. Exactly what this means with respect to the student and his locker is not yet fully clear.

A "search" is made where the school officials cause the student to reveal or uncover something otherwise covered, and a command to "empty your pockets" is a search within the meaning of the term. However, a student may be asked to cooperate; if he does so, he may waive his rights, where his cooperation voluntarily uncovers incriminating evidence against him. The Fourth Amendment does not prohibit search, it merely prohibits "unreasonable" search. From *Marlar v. Bill* (Case No. 41, *supra*) it has been held that the teacher may reasonably search young children if the search is to vindicate their honor in a situation such as that outlined in the case.

Evidence obtained in an illegal search may not be introduced in court, hence, is useless although it "has the goods on the culprit." It behooves those who are conducting the search, therefore, to move carefully so that the evidence obtained may be legally introduced as produced by a legal, rather than an illegal, search.

A good discussion of this problem is given in Lawrence Knowles, "Crime Investigation in the Schools: Its Constitutional Dimensions," 4 *Journal of Family Law* 151, 1964. Such topics as consequences of an unconstitutional search and police interrogation of school students are covered in the article.

Under the "suppression" doctrine, illegally seized evidence cannot be introduced, but it is doubtful if this practice, contrary to what many persons thought following the *Miranda* decision, reached a point of endangering public safety. In 1964, Chief Justice Warren E. Burger, then Judge Burger of the U.S. Court of Appeals in Washington, D.C., traced the suppression doctrine back to 1886 when the Supreme Court banned evidence consisting of a man's private papers in *Boyd v. United States.* In subsequent and often conflicting opinions, the Judge noted that more and more "technicalities" are making the search and seizure area a thicket "of considerable density." That this would inevitably apply to student affairs (such as dormitory rooms, and other educational affairs) was obvious.

Although applicable to criminal procedures, the rules applying to search and seizure of students and their lockers were laid down by the Supreme Court first in *Escobedo v. Illinois,* and later in the *Miranda* decision. Three rules were applied that have implications for school personnel:

1. If a person is to be subjected to interrogation, he must first be informed in clear and unequivocal terms that he has the right to remain silent —the warning of the right to remain silent must be accompanied by the explanation that anything said can and will be used against the individual in court.

2. The right to have counsel present at the interrogation is indispensable to the protection of the Fifth Amendment privilege to choose between silence and speech. Failure to have a lawyer does not waive the right to have one. An individual must be told of his right to counsel and reminded that the state will foot the bill if he is indigent.

3. If the interrogation continues without the presence of an attorney, and a statement is taken, heavy burden rests upon the Government to demonstrate that the defendant knowingly and intelligently waived his privilege against self-incrimination and his right to counsel. Whenever a person held in custody indicates "in any manner" that he does not wish to be interrogated, the police may not question him.

In schools, however, a distinction is evident between proceedings leading to a criminal indictment, and a mere disciplinary inquiry into the student's activities. The key here seems to be the extent of the potential punishment—where there is a likelihood that the student may be held to a criminal charge, or dismissed from the school, his rights must be protected. On the other hand, where the objective of the inquiry is to determine whether a school rule has been broken, and the penalty is such that it will not deprive the student of his right to attend school (detention is an example of this type of punishment) more latitude in the investigation is allowable. In general, the more serious and long-lasting the possible penalties to be assessed, the more careful must the investigators be in conducting their search.

43   *School's Right to Control Membership in Secret Societies*

Instead of suspending or expelling students for membership in certain secret societies, the board of Columbus, Ohio prohibited students from participating in athletic, literary, military, musical, dramatic, service, scientific, or scholastic activities as members of these clubs. Also the high school student who was a member of such clubs was declared ineligible to hold student office or to receive rewards. School officials testified that the clubs had a divisive influence on the school and tended to undermine the authority of the school personnel. Meetings were held off school property in private homes, and it was contended that the organizations were really not fraternities and that the board had no control over outside activities such as these. Club members held positions in various school programs and activities in numbers out of proportion to the total school membership.

Relief Sought: To enjoin enforcement of a board rule making membership in certain organizations a bar to participation in extra-curricular activities.

Issue: Does the board of education have the authority to prohibit students in public high schools from affiliating with fraternities, sororities, and other social clubs under penalty of rendering such students ineligible to participate in certain extra-curricular activities?

Holding of the Trial Court: For superintendent and the board

Holding of the Appellate Court: Affirmed

Reasoning

The board of education is vested with broad discretionary powers in adopting policy for the government, management, and discipline of the schools. Such regulations as this one, even in the absence of statute permitting them to do so, are a legitimate exercise of the board's powers. Such a regulation does not deprive pupils of privileges, when in the opinion of school authorities, such organizations have a deleterious effect and are found to be inimical to the best interests of the school.

Significance

Even in the absence of an enabling statute the board of education has the power to control outside organizations, such as secret fraternities, sororities, and other social clubs for students by denying their members the right to participate in extra-curricular activities where it is determined that the clubs in question have a deleterious influence on the school and over its control.

CASE CITATION: *Holroyd v. Eibling, 188 N.E.2d 797 (Ohio 1962)*

AUTHOR'S COMMENTARY

The nexus of the issue of the cases involving secret societies in the public schools is whether the board may sufficiently control such organizations or whether they are indeed "outside" organizations *ultra vires* the control of the board. In *Wilson v. Board of Education,* 137 Ill.App. 192, the question of secret societies in schools was considered.

> There may be a contrariety of opinion as to whether secret societies in schools among pupils are beneficial or harmful to either the pupil or the cause of education. In such condition, who shall decide whether the pupils should be encouraged or not in making affiliation with any of them? The courts or the board? It makes no difference which of them shall control so far as affecting the ultimate conclusion is concerned, for the courts have been quite outspoken in their condemnation of such societies in schools as hurtful to the pupil and detrimental to his educational progress. Even if it were otherwise, if the rule is reasonable and equal in its operation, the courts cannot impose their judgment or opinion contrary or in opposition to that of the board, which, in promulgating such rules, acts judicially.

In *Bradford v. Board of Education of City of San Francisco,* 121 Pac. 929, 1912 the constitutionality of a California law was in issue. The act "prevented the formation and prohibited the existence of secret, oath-bound fraternities in the public schools." The court upheld its constitutionality in a case in which a girl was suspended from the public school because she had joined a Greek-letter sorority in violation of the statute. "The privilege of attending the public schools of the state," said the court on that occasion, "is not a privilege or immunity covered under the Fourteenth Amendment. It necessarily follows, therefore, that no person can lawfully demand admission as a pupil in any public school simply because of the mere status of citizenship."

The right of school officials to control membership in secret, oath-bound societies applies regardless of these facts: 1) the parents wish their children to belong and often offer their homes as meeting places for the club meetings; 2) the meetings are held off school grounds and outside school hours; and 3) there may be little evidence of a concrete nature to indicate that the organizations are a threat to the board's authority over the schools. The courts will not interfere with the board's control over these organizations if the board can reasonably infer that their existence is inimical to the pupil or to the board's control over the school and its students.

In *Hughes v. Caddo Parish School Board,* 323 U.S. 685, La. 1945, the United States Supreme Court held that schools may with statutory authority control membership in secret societies in public schools. There are several dozen lesser court decisions which parallel this higher court decision, some of which hold that the board has such powers even in the absence of a state statute giving boards such authority. A test of whether such organizations are constitutionally protected under the First Amendment has not been found, but it is conceivable that "the right to peaceably assemble" may be involved. The question is far from settled law at this writing.

44   *Vaccination as a Condition of School Attendance*

Ordinances of the City of San Antonio provided that no child or other person should attend a public school without first presenting a certificate of vaccination. School officials excluded Rosalyn Zucht from school because she did not have the required certificate and refused to submit to vaccination. Thereupon suit was brought to gain her admission. The plaintiffs claimed that there was then no occasion for requiring vaccination, and that the ordinance in question deprived her of her liberty by making vaccination compulsory.

Relief Sought: Injunctive relief against enforcement of a school rule and a writ of mandamus to compel plaintiff's admission to school

Issue: Is a rule by the board requiring vaccination as a condition of public school attendance contrary to the personal rights provided in the Fourteenth Amendment?

Holding of the Trial Court: For defendant school officials

Holding of the United States Supreme Court: Affirmed

Reasoning

A city ordinance is a law of the State and it is within the police power of a State to provide for compulsory vaccination. A State may, consistent with the

Federal Constitution, delegate to a municipality authority to determine under what conditions health regulations shall become operative. In the exercise of police power, reasonable classification may be freely applied and the regulation is not violative of the equal protection clause of the Fourteenth Amendment. The Supreme Court can have jurisdiction only if there is a substantial constitutional question involved, as here. But this is not a new constitutional issue of substance. We ruled on this in *Jacobson v. Massachusetts*, 197 U.S. 11, Mass. 1905, and we see no reason to change our finding in that case.

Significance

A state through its municipalities has the power to require vaccination of its school children as a condition of attending public schools, and such an exercise of the police power of the State does not deprive a person of his "equal protection of the law" rights under the Fourteenth Amendment.

CASE CITATION: *Zucht v. King, 260 U.S. 174 (Texas 1922)*

AUTHOR'S COMMENTARY

The question of compulsory vaccination balances the right of the individual freedom on the one hand over against the right of the general public to be healthy and safe on the other. The United States Supreme Court has indicated that under these circumstances, individual freedom must give way to the greater good to the greater numbers.

In 1905, the Supreme Court dealt with the case of *Jacobson v. Massachusetts*, 197 U.S. 11, Mass. 1905. At issue was a statute of that state providing that a city or town board of health, if it deemed it necessary for public health or safety, could require vaccination, or re-vaccination, of all inhabitants thereof. Although the vaccination was free, one Jacobson resisted it on the grounds that such a statute violated the guarantees included in the Fourteenth Amendment, and that he had previously suffered seriously from vaccination. Nevertheless, the statute was upheld by the Supreme Court. Plaintiff Jacobson, said the Court, should have filed for an exception under the law, rather than challenging its constitutionality. Since the law provided for such exceptions, and the Massachusetts Supreme Court said it was not mandatory if it would endanger any person's health or life, the Supreme Court could not find the statute unconstitutional.

In the earlier cases, immunization was against smallpox, but in 1963 the Supreme Court of Ohio had before it the question of whether a school board could also require immunization against other diseases, in this case poliomyelitis, pertussis and tetanus in addition to smallpox. *State ex rel. Mack v. Bd. of Educ. of Covington,* 204 N.E.2d 86, Ohio 1963. Although the parents presented a written statement of objection to the rule the board refused to admit their child because he was not immunized. The court held that such a decision was within the legal powers of the local board of education.

Sometimes the objection to vaccinating public school children is based on religious grounds. In a case which arose in North Carolina, a parent was convicted of failure to vaccinate his child and send him to school. The Supreme Court of North Carolina held that the question of whether the father was justified by the teachings of his religious organization was for the jury to decide on the evidence. Letters from the officers of the religious order concerning the organization's teachings with respect to immunization did not show that the organization had an official stand against vaccination. In ordering a new trial, the court said that despite North Carolina law to the contrary,

> In our opinion, it is not necessary for a religious organization to forbid vaccination in order for its teachings to come within the meaning of the statute and to authorize the exclusion sought; that it is for the jury under proper instructions to determine whether or not the evidence concerning the teachings of the Miracle Revival Fellowship is such that the defendant was justified in his position against vaccination and the immunization of his child. . . . Defendant is entitled to a new trial on the counts charging him with failure to have his child immunized against smallpox and poliomyelitis. *State v. Miday,* 140 S.E.2d 325, N.C. 1965.

Does the absence of an epidemic change the legal question involving vaccination of school children? In Arkansas, a school board requirement that all students must be vaccinated as a condition of school attendance was challenged on the grounds that among other things, there had been no smallpox in the county for more than fifty years. *Wright v. DeWitt School Dist.,* 385 S.W.2d 644, Ark. 1965. Said the court:

> It is well settled that smallpox is a contagious disease which is a scourge to mankind. . . . Our courts, both state and federal, take judicial notice of the very nature of this loathsome disease and that it presents a clear and ever present danger which is best controlled by health measures such as the one in question. . . . The courts are not required to listen to conflicting evidence as to the need of vaccination against smallpox.

Another parent challenged the compulsory vaccination rule as an inva-sion of his right to practice religion freely. *Prince v. Massachusetts,* 321 U.S. 158, Mass. 1944.

> Neither rights of religion nor rights of parenthood are beyond limitation. Acting to guard the general interest in youth's well being, the state as *parens patriae* may restrict the parent's control by requiring school attendance, regulating or prohibiting the child's labor, and in many other ways. Its authority is not nullified merely because the parent grounds his claim to control the child's course of conduct on religion or conscience. Thus, he cannot claim freedom from compulsory vaccination for the child more than for himself on religious grounds. *The right to practice religion freely does not include liberty to expose the community or the child to communicable disease or the latter to ill health or death.* (Emphasis supplied.)

Thus, in the realm of compulsory vaccination for children, the rule is that the common good must transcend the individual's constitutional rights. As Justice Field of the United States Supreme Court wrote in 1890:

> But the possession and enjoyment of all rights are subject to such reasonable conditions as may be deemed by the governing authority of the country essential to the safety, health, peace, good order, and morals of the community. Even liberty itself, the greatest of all rights, is not unrestricted license to act according to one's own will. It is only freedom from restraint under conditions essential to the equal enjoyment of the same right by others. It is then liberty regulated by law. *Crowley v. Christensen,* 137 U.S. 86, 1890.

45   *Inducing Children to Play Hooky*

On June 1, 1964, a regular school day, a "substantial number of children of school age" were encouraged to engage in picketing with the respon-dent and other adults at Junior High School # 136 and # 139, Manhattan, to demonstrate objectives which could not later be clearly stated by those children who testified. In addition, the respondent was designated as the person "in charge" of the group in a basement dwelling before the demonstration. When school attendance officials tried to get the children back to the school the respondent ordered them to leave. The respondent had no legal relationship to the children involved but held that the right to protest by boycott was legal.

> *Relief Sought:* Restraint for violation of the Education Code of New York

Issue: Is one who keeps children out of school to dramatize conditions in the schools and who interferes with attendance officials subject to criminal proceedings?

Holding of the Trial Court: For the people. Respondent sentenced to ten days in city jail, which was suspended on condition that respondent refrain from further violation of the Education Law

Holding of the Appellate Court: Affirmed

Reasoning

The efforts of the school system to effect regular school attendance should not be interfered with even if the objectives are laudable. Evidence showed that the respondent did harbor the students in said basement premises and did interfere with the officials of the bureau of attendance in the performance of their duties. While the courts recognize that in some cases the right to boycott is protected (Montgomery, Alabama bus cases) they will not condone the boycotting of the schools.

Significance

The social importance of the schools is such in our culture that the state has set up schools for its preservation. The people are entitled to an uninterrupted and on-going public school system, and nothing should be allowed to interfere with it in any way, even though the cause is a good one.

CASE CITATION: *People v. Anonymous, 253 N.Y.S.2d 934 (N.Y. 1964)*

46 Dress Code in a Public High School

Thomas Breen, 16 and James Anton, 17 were given the choice of getting haircuts or being expelled from the Williams Bay High School. They chose instead to ask the federal court to declare the following board regulation unconstitutional: "Hair shall be washed, combed and worn so it does not hang below the collar line in back, and over the ears on the side and must be above the eyebrows. Boys should be clean shaven; long sideburns are out." District Court Judge James E. Doyle held that "to deny plaintiffs access to a public high school is to inflict upon each of them irreparable injury for which no remedy at law is adequate. I make this finding by taking judicial notice of the social, economic, and psychological value and importance today of receiving a public education through twelfth grade."

Relief Sought: Reinstatement and injunction against enforcement of a school rule

Issue: Does a board regulation limiting dress and appearance of students as applied to plaintiffs violate the Constitution of the United States?

Holding of the District Court: For plaintiffs

Holding of the United States Court of Appeals: Affirmed

Holding of the United States Supreme Court: Certiorari denied June 1, 1970

Reasoning

The freedom of an adult male or female to present himself or herself physically to the world in the manner of his or her choice is a highly protected freedom. . . . For the state to impair this freedom, in the absence of a compelling subordinating interest in doing so, would offend a widely shared concept of human dignity, would assault personality and individuality, would undermine identity, and would invade human "being". . . . It would deprive a man or a woman of liberty without due process of law in violation of the Fourteenth Amendment. The question is does it apply to these plaintiffs? The students who are subjected to these (board) regulations do not vote in school elections; political redress of their grievances is not open to them; theirs is a situation in which judicial vindication of constitutional protections has not been considered particularly appropriate. . . . It is time to broaden the constitutional community by including within its protections younger people whose claim to dignity matches that of their elders. (Citing *In re Gault,* 387 U.S. 1, Ariz. 1967.)

Significance

The refusal of the U.S. Supreme Court to grant certiorari in *Breen v. Kahl* is puzzling, since it sets up a direct conflict with the Circuit Court's decision in *Ferrell v. Dallas Ind. School District,* 392 F.2d 697, Texas 1969, which upheld a school district's haircut rule and on which certiorari was also denied.

CASE CITATION: *Breen v. Kahl, 296 F.Supp. 702 (Wisc. 1969)*

AUTHOR'S COMMENTARY

The Supreme Judicial Court of Massachusetts was the first court of last resort in a state to decide a question of the appearance of a high school male student. In 1965, in *Leonard v. School Committee of Attleboro,* 212 N.E.2d

468, Mass. 1965, the question was whether a board restriction on haircuts infringed on the basic rights of parents. Said the court on that occasion, in upholding the rule in question:

> We are mindful that the regulation of haircuts may affect the private and personal lives of students more substantially than do restrictions regarding dress. Whereas the latter need not operate beyond the school premises, the former will inevitably do so. Therefore the plaintiff contends that the challenged ruling is an invasion of family privacy touching matters occurring while he is at home and within the exclusive control of his parents. . . . Here, the domain of family privacy must give way in so far as a regulation reasonably calculated to maintain school discipline may affect it. *The rights of other students, and the interest of teachers, administrators, and the community at large in a well run and efficient school system are paramount.* (Emphasis added.)

Despite the claim by plaintiff that his hair style was essential to his public image as a jazz musician, the court sustained the board's right to adopt a regulation of the type under question.

The decision in favor of the board in *Leonard* is representative of the early position of the courts with regard to school regulation of hair fashions. Prior to *Tinker v. Des Moines School Board,* 393 U.S. 503, Iowa, 1969, Case No. 21, *supra* the majority of the cases were in favor of the board of education. In *Ferrell v. Dallas Independent School District,* 392 F.2d 697, Texas, 1968, for example, the court did not reject the contention that hair fashion was a form of expression protected by the Constitution, but did hold that the school board has a legitimate interest in subordinating that right. Since *Ferrell,* however, two federal district courts within the Fifth Circuit have granted relief to similarly situated students on the ground that there was no evidence that their hair styles materially and substantially interfered with the requirements of appropriate discipline in the operation of the school. See *Calbillo v. San Jacinto Junior College,* 305 F.Supp. 857, Texas, 1969, and *Griffin v. Tatum,* 300 F.Supp. 60, Ala. 1969. *Tinker,* in effect, established the principle of law that, absent a factual showing of material and substantial disruption of discipline, a school board may not infringe on a student's exercise of his fundamental liberties. One could conjecture that all hair style cases after *Tinker* would rely heavily upon this decision for its conclusion.

In *Neuhaus v. Torrey,* U.S. Dist. Court, N. D. of Calif., No. C-70 304, March 3, 1970, the court held that exclusion of boys with long hair from athletic competition solely on that basis alone is a constitutional infringement of a fundamental liberty, and cannot be enforced. Said the court:

Coach Troppman testified that, in his view, a regulation requiring athletes to part their hair in the middle would be unreasonable. But such a rule would meet all of the criteria advanced for justifying the hair regulation (e. g., uniformity and discipline) but would be less an infringement on plaintiffs' right to privacy. A "middle-part" rule would at least have this advantage for plaintiffs. They could part their hair as they pleased when they left school. But they cannot wear their hair longer by night and on weekends and shorter during the day. The haircut regulation controls their appearance every minute of the day.

In the *Breen* case *supra,* Judge Doyle spoke to the claim that long hair was a distraction in school:

With respect to the "distraction" factor, the showing of this record consists of expressions of opinion by several educational administrators that an abnormal appearance of one student distracts others. There is no direct testimony that such distraction has occurred. . . . From the testimony of the educational administrators, it appears that the absence of such amplification (proof) is not accidental; it arises from the absence of factual data which might prove the amplification.

To the claim that students with long hair were more likely to perform less effectively than those with shorter hair, the court had this to say:

With respect to the "comparative performance" factor, this record is equally barren. The expert opinions are fewer than those on the distraction factor. No empirical findings are offered. No hard facts are adduced even from a limited sample to demonstrate that the academic performance of male students with long hair is inferior to that of male students with short hair, or that the former are less active or less effective in extra-curricular activities.

Nor was the court convinced that long hair in itself is injurious to health. In concluding that school officials had fallen "far short" in their attempts to show the ill effects of long hair and the justification for the rule in question, the court castigated the board for not bearing the "substantial burden of justification" which was necessary when the state attempts to demonstrate "that a compelling and legitimate governmental purpose will be served by the exclusion."

It thus appears from these cases that no hard and fast rule on hair styles in school can be postulated, since each case must rest upon its own merits. It is not impossible to show that a board rule controlling a fundamental human right is necessary in any one instance, but the burden is "substantial" and so far no board has been able to prove to the satisfaction of the court, at least since *Tinker,* that "a compelling and legitimate governmental purpose" outweighs an individual student's right to exercise his fundamental freedoms. When these two come into conflict, the courts seem prone to balance the scales in favor of the individual, unless a clear and present danger is evident, or the government can clearly demonstrate the need for the enforcement of such a ruling.

What this means is that the board must base its claim that the rule is necessary on more than simple distaste for long hair.

47   Immodest Dress in School

Appellant's daughter was suspended from a public school because she refused to participate in the physical education program. Reason given for her refusal was that the costume prescribed by the school officials was immodest and sinful according to the religious beliefs of the girl and her parents. The school officials made certain adjustments by offering to allow her to wear clothing which she would consider suitable, and agreed she would not have to perform any exercises that seemed to her or her parents to be immodest, but she would be required to attend the class. She still refused to attend the class, and was subsequently suspended from school. She sued for readmittance.

Relief Sought: Admission to a public school

Issue: May a girl who refuses according to her religious beliefs to wear an abbreviated gym suit in her gymnasium classes be legally suspended from a public school?

Holding of the Trial Court: For defendant board of education

Holding of the Appellate Court: Affirmed

Reasoning

No constitutional right is abridged by the requirement that a student must wear certain clothing while engaged in activities within the school. Every precaution had been taken to insure that the course be conducted in a manner consistent with modesty and good taste. Based upon previous cases (cited) the court ruled that attendance at a state institution is voluntary, and therefore a pupil cannot refuse to comply with a reasonable rule lawfully required and still demand readmission. Such regulations as those relating to compulsory vaccination, and the obligation to bear arms have been upheld as reasonable exercises of the state's police power. Every reasonable concession has been made to the appellant in this case. Nor is the appellant "a speckled bird," subject to the contumely of her fellow students when she is placed in the presence of others whose dress and behavior is contrary to her scruples. All citizens insofar as they hold views different from the majority of their fellows are subject to such inconveniences. And this is especially true of those who hold religious or moral beliefs which are looked upon with disdain by the majority. It is precisely every citizen's right to be "a speckled bird" that our constitutions, state and federal, seek to insure. And solace for the embarrassment that is attendant upon holding such beliefs must be found by the individual citizen in his own moral courage and strength of conviction, and not in a court of law.

Significance

A student may not be required to participate in exercises which she or her parents consider immodest in immodest apparel, nor is she required to wear the prescribed outfit. But the student is required to attend the class.

CASE CITATION: *Mitchell v. McCall, 143 So.2d 629 (Ala. 1962)*

48   Freedom Buttons

A number of high school students in an all-Negro high school in Mississippi appeared in school wearing circular buttons, 1½ inches in diameter, containing the wording "One Man One Vote" around the perimeter with "SNCC" inscribed in the center. The principal told the students they could not wear the buttons in school because they did not have any bearing on the students' education and would only "cause a commotion." Some students who continued to display the buttons were given the choice of removing them or being sent home. Most chose to go home and the principal thereupon suspended them for one week. The students sought to clarify their rights in court, maintaining that wearing the buttons was a mode of free speech protected under the First Amendment.

Relief Sought: Injunctive relief against enforcement of a school regulation forbidding the wearing of freedom buttons in school

> *Issue:* Is enforcing a school regulation forbidding school children from wearing freedom buttons a denial of constitutional rights?
>
> *Holding of the Trial Court:* For the school board
>
> *Holding of the Circuit Court of Appeals:* Reversed with directions to invalidate the rule

Reasoning

We wish to make it clear that we do not applaud any attempt to undermine the authority of the school. We must also emphasize that school officials cannot ignore expressions of feeling with which they do not wish to contend. They cannot infringe on their students' right to free and unrestricted expression as guaranteed them under the First Amendment to the Constitution where the exercise of such rights in the school buildings and school grounds do not materially and substantially interfere with the requirements of appropriate discipline in the operation of the school. On former occasions, students wore "Beatle buttons" and buttons containing the initials of students, and these were not proscribed. In an all-Negro high school such as this, the right to communicate a matter of vital public concern is embraced in the First Amendment right to freedom of speech and therefore is clearly protected against infringement by state officials. Particularly, the Fourteenth Amendment protects the First Amendment rights of school children against unreasonable rules and regulations imposed by school authorities.

Significance

School children have the right under the First and Fourteenth Amendments to communicate ideas through the wearing of freedom buttons and other buttons where their actions do not cause a disruption in the school. This right is further supported by the Supreme Court's decision in the *Tinker* case (see Case No. 21).

CASE CITATION: *Burnside v. Byars, 363 F.2d 744 (Miss. 1966)*

49   Freedom Buttons

Plaintiffs were Negro high school students in Mississippi who were suspended from school for the balance of the year for causing an unusual degree of commotion, boisterous conduct, collision with the rights of other students, and using discourteous remarks to school officials. Students distributed freedom buttons to other students in the corridors of the building and pinned buttons on some even though they did not want them. One of the students tried to pin a button on a younger child who began crying. This caused a state of confusion, disrupted classroom instruction, and resulted in a general breakdown of order and discipline. The principal told the assembled students in the cafeteria that they were forbidden to wear the buttons at school. In defiance of this rule, about 200 students showed up next day wearing the buttons, and suspension resulted.

Relief Sought: Injunctive relief against enforcement of a school regulation forbidding the wearing of freedom buttons in school

Issue: Is enforcing a school regulation forbidding school children from wearing freedom buttons a denial of constitutional rights?

Holding of the Trial Court: For defendant board of education

Holding of the Appellate Court: Affirmed

Reasoning

The issue here is identical to the case immediately above (see Case No. 48). The difference however is the fact that in the present case there was a disturbance which the school authorities had a right, if not a duty, to quell. The students were warned at least three times that they would be suspended if they wore the buttons to school, yet they refused to refrain from doing so. They ignored the rule, and in leaving, they created a general disturbance by urging other students to leave with them. Under these circumstances, the suspensions were valid, the key difference being that here there was a disturbance whereas in the case which was similar there was no disturbance accompanying the wearing of the buttons. The action of suspending the students was necessary in order to maintain order in classrooms and in the halls and to protect the rights of other students. "The proper operation of the school system is one of the highest and most fundamental responsibilities of the state."

Significance

The wearing of freedom buttons or other evidences of free speech may be banned in instances where their use leads to a disruption of the orderly routine of the school.

CASE CITATION: *Blackwell v. Issaquena County Board of Education, 363 F.2d 749 (Miss. 1966)*

50   Expulsion from School

Plaintiffs on behalf of their son sought his reinstatement after expulsion from high school for intemperate speech and mutilation of the flag, constituting "behavior which was inimicable to the welfare, safety, or morals of other pupils." A Colorado statute, Section 123-20-7, Colorado Revised Statutes, 1963, sets forth specifically the grounds and the only grounds upon which a child may be expelled from public school in the state.

Relief Sought: Reinstatement to school after expulsion

Issue: May the board expel a high school student who during a classroom speech allegedly tore up an American flag?

Holding of the Court: For plaintiffs

Reasoning

The Colorado statutes set forth the grounds for expulsion. Any expulsion based on any other grounds is illegal. The burden of proof rests with the board to prove that plaintiffs' son committed the act alleged, which they did. They must also prove that his behavior was "harmful to the welfare, safety or morals of the other pupils." This they failed to do. The board produced no evidence whatsoever that the welfare, safety, or morals of any pupil was harmed by what (the boy) said or did, or even that the class was distracted or the school disrupted by what he did. Some of the students were no doubt stunned or shocked or offended by what they heard, but in my mind behavior which only shocks, stuns or offends falls far short of behavior (inimical) of one's welfare, safety, or morals, and therefore for these reasons the Court finds that the order of expulsion fails to comply with the School Attendance Law of 1963. Because of my ruling that no legal grounds existed for this boy's expulsion, I find it unnecessary to consider whether the board followed legal procedures in going about his dismissal. I recognize that a board faced with a situation of this kind is concerned about acting promptly and quickly, and I don't question the integrity or fairmindedness of the board, but I do quite honestly have serious doubts about whether the most fundamental requirements of procedural due process were followed by the school board. And I am also aware of the fact that there could well be serious First Amendment right of free speech issues involved in this case, but again I do not feel it necessary to go into that because of the determination which I have made that there were no legal grounds under the statute for dismissal.

Significance

A school may not silence its students simply "to avoid the discomfort and unpleasantness that always accompany an unpopular viewpoint."

CASE CITATION: *Canfield v. School District No. 8, Proceeding No. J-842, District Court Within and For the County of El Paso and State of Colorado, April 16, 1970*

AUTHOR'S COMMENTARY

School boards look defensive when called on in court to "bear the burden of proof" as here that a student's behavior or speech has been

inimicable to the welfare, safety, or morals of the other students, or that a
student's behavior has been disruptive of the educative process. It could well
be argued that this *is* "the educative process" itself—learning to live as
Americans in a democratic form of government. The school board, as a part
of that government, must scrupulously avoid heavy-handed methods which
in court might be construed as depriving citizens of their constitutional
rights to exercise fundamental liberties under all conditions.

Judge Gallagher in the *Canfield* case, *supra,* pointed out that while he
did not approve of the student's behavior ("I think he exercised extremely
poor judgment in this instance") nevertheless he must uphold the law which
permits such displays of viewpoint even though it may be distasteful to the
community as well as the board of education. Punishing the child because of
his behavior in school solves nothing. "It seems to me that the least satisfactory way to open a child's mind is to deny him an education," the court
concluded.

In setting aside the board's resolution to expel, the court directed the
board to take appropriate action "to assist him in making up the work lost
by his expulsion."

In another expulsion case, *Naranjo v. Board of Consolidated School
District No. 8,* Civil Action No. 6975, District Court Within and For the
County of Rio Grande and State of Colorado, May 26, 1970, the same
Colorado statute was under interpretation by the court, although here the
grounds chosen by the board were "continued willful disobedience or open
and persistent defiance of proper authority." CRS § 123-20-7(b), 1963.
Following an altercation at a track meet, plaintiff was one of two senior boys
expelled by the board. He sought reinstatement in court, and his suit was
successful. While agreeing that the established policy of the board to suspend
students for three days was justified, it was not justified in expelling boys
who would soon graduate on the basis of this one incident. Said the court:
"It is a little like using a sledge hammer to kill a gnat."

> This boy was about to leave school. Obviously, he would not be
> around any more. The Court regrets being placed in the position of
> second-guessing the Board, but I have no other alternative but to find
> that the Board has abused its discretion in this case; that its initial
> suspension is approved and was proper in view of its own policy, but that
> there is no evidence to support its second action of expulsion.

On the matter of "willful disobedience" and "persistent defiance of
proper authority" the court had this to say:

> The statutory ground, "continued willful disobedience or open and
> persistent defiance of proper authority"—that could include fighting, I

suppose, but it will take a lot more fighting than we have here, gentlemen. . . . Now, "willful disobedience" has a well-known legal meaning that has been construed in three or four decisions that I have found, and it involves a wrongful or perverse disposition. I haven't even seen any disobedience here. All I have seen is a school-boy fight. . . . Now, "continued" also has a well-known legal meaning. It means prolonged, without interruption in sequence; in other words, uninterrupted or unbroken. And a verbal rumble in February and a fight in May doesn't qualify for "uninterrupted willful disobedience." . . . "Persistent defiance" seems to have a legal meaning, too, and it seems a chronic, constant and continuous defiance. I am unable to find that that exists here either.

. . . Accordingly, the judgment of this court will be that the order of expulsion of the Board will be set aside and the child ordered readmitted to school.

PART FOUR

Tort Liability of
the School Officials and Staff

Part Four

Tort Liability of
the School Officials and Staff

"*All of the paths leading to the origin of governmental tort immunity converge on Russell v. The Men of Devon (1788),*" said the Supreme Court of Minnesota in 1962. "This product of the English common law was left on our doorstep to become the putative ancestor of a long line of American cases beginning with *Mower v. Leicester* (1812)." But, there is evidence that the doctrine which holds that school districts, as subdivisions of state government, are immune to tort liability is on the way out in this country.

The abrogation of the tort immunity of governmental subdivisions may be accomplished either by legislative enactment or by judicial fiat. Some state supreme courts are reluctant to act where they believe it is the duty of the legislature to abrogate tort immunity of state agencies, as for example, the Supreme Court of Colorado when considering whether a school district should be held to account for an injury to a basketball player:

> We have held repeatedly that if liability is to arise against a governmental agency for the negligent acts of its servants engaged in a governmental function, this liability, heretofore unknown to the law of the state, must be a creation of the legislative branch of the government. . . . It is not the function of the judiciary to create confusion and instability in well settled law, nor is it within the province of judges to refuse to apply firmly established principles of law simply because those rules do not conform to the individual judge's philosophical notions as to what the law should be. . . . Courts are not arbiters of public policy. *Tesone v. School District,* 384 P.2d 82 (Colo. 1963).

Nevertheless, the doctrine was promulgated by the courts, and handed down through *stare decisis* (let the decision stand). When the Iowa Supreme Court upheld immunity in 1966, the Iowa legislature acted by passing a statute abrogating the immunity of school districts in that state in 1967. Other states have abrogated the immunity rule either by legislation or by judicial action. The reader should become familiar with the status of the doctrine in his own state in order to determine the liability of the district to damages for its acts of negligence.

The immunity which school districts (as subdivisions of state government) enjoy, however, does not extend to school district employees. Like all other citizens, school teachers, principals, and non-certificated personnel working for the school district must stand to account for their own tortious (actionable) wrongs against others.

This section of the present volume deals with the question of the liability of the school district, its officials, and its employees. Seventeen actual cases are briefed here, and several others introduced to illustrate the principles of law governing this section of the book. The reader will note a trend toward the gradual elimination of the governmental immunity doctrine, due not only to the availability of cheap liability insurance, but also to the need to protect innocent parties from the injuries which inevitably come about through the operation of a large, complex and restless enterprise, the operation of the public school systems of the land.

These same districts are engaged, as they by right ought to be, in their intended function, namely, the education of the young. This function, which is called its "governmental" function, generally affords the district with some protection merely because of the nature of the enterprise itself, i.e., the school district is a subdivision engaged in the education of the young, and if someone is injured thereby, he has less standing to complain than if he is injured through a non-governmental activity. Such functions as athletics, trips, plays, summer recreation programs, and large in-gatherings of people are not directly related to the avowed function of the school, and hence a larger liability attaches to them. These activities are generally referred to as "the school's proprietary functions," which will be explained more clearly in this section of the book. (See the AUTHOR'S COMMENTARY following Case 54 for a further discussion of this point of law.)

51   Tort Immunity Doctrine

This was an action upon the case against the men dwelling in the County of Devon to recover satisfaction for an injury done to the waggon of the plaintiff in consequence of a bridge being out of repair, which ought to have been repaired by the county; to which two of the inhabitants, appeared, and demurred generally. Defendants in support of the demurrer insisted that by the laws of this kingdom no civil action can be maintained against the inhabitants of a county at large for an injury sustained by an individual in consequence of a breach of their public duty. Parties to the defense, being unorganized, are not corporations, but individuals, and no act of Parliament has made the inhabitants of a county at large liable in a case. The inhabitants of a county are a fluctuating body, and before judgment obtained, other men may have come to reside in the county, when the whole damages may be levied on such innocent persons. No man shall be liable for the negligence of another.

Relief Sought: Damages for injuries to his wagon by reason of a bridge being out of repair

Issue: Are all the male inhabitants of a county liable for damages to plaintiff's "waggon" by reason of a bridge being out of repair?

Holding of the Trial Court: For the defendants, Men of Devon

Reasoning

This action cannot lie because: 1) to permit it would lead to "an infinity of actions," 2) there was no precedent for attempting such a suit, 3) only the legislature should impose liability of this kind, 4) even if defendants are to be considered a corporation or quasi-corporation, there is no fund out of which to satisfy the claim, 5) neither law nor reason supports the action, 6) there is a strong presumption that what has never been done cannot be done, and 7) although there is a legal principle which permits a remedy for every injury resulting from the negligence of another, a more acceptable principle is "that it is better that an individual should sustain an injury than that the public should suffer an inconvenience." Every reason here given is born of expediency, yet this case became ruling case law in this country for many years, and still obtains (tort immunity doctrine) in many states in 1970. No mention is made of the so-called "the King can do no wrong" principle upon which the outcome of this case is supposedly based. The familiar cry of the judiciary, "let the legislative branch take heed and do something about this type of situation . . ." rings a bell, because many of the state supreme courts in recent years have made similar admonitions upon their legislatures.

Significance

Russell and his "waggon" set the precedent in America for many years: the state is immune to suit for its negligent torts (actionable wrongs) because, being engaged in a governmental function, it cannot be held to the high standard of care expected of individuals. This "governmental tort immunity doctrine" successfully shielded school boards, and other subdivisions of state government, from suit for liability and is still the rule in about half of the states. The trend, however, is for the state to abrogate the rule, either by means of statute, or by judicial fiat in cases where employees of the state have by their negligence brought injury to third parties.

CASE CITATION: *Russell v. The Men of Devon, 100 Eng. Rep. 359, 2 T.R. 667 (1788)*

AUTHOR'S COMMENTARY

In *Mower v. The Inhabitants of Leicester,* 9 Mass. 247, 1812, the owner and proprietor of a public stagecoach brought an action to recover damages against the town of Leicester on much the grounds used by Russell against the Men of Devon. There was a large hole between the stones in the bridge in Leicester, and one of the horses stepped through it and was severely injured so that he later died. Towns are by law supposed to keep their bridges and roads in good condition. Leicester was a corporation, capable of being sued and of suing in its own behalf. The law provided for double damages to one who suffered an injury through negligence on the part of a Massachusetts town. But towns are not corporations, in the real sense, but *quasi-*corporations, created by the state for purposes of public policy, to further a state purpose. They are created by the legislature and are subject by the common law to an indictment for the neglect of duties enjoined on them, but "are not liable to an action for such neglect, unless the action be given by some statute." This principle of law is discussed in *Russell v. Men of Devon,* cited at the bar, "and the reasoning there is conclusive against the action."

Hence, beginning in 1812 with *Mower,* the American courts drew on the governmental tort immunity doctrine to protect governmental subdivisions as a matter of policy. This principle was governing law for well over one hundred and fifty years in the United States, and still obtains in about twenty-five states.

Regardless of whether the school district is or is not immune, liability for the district's actionable wrongs (torts) attaches only in those cases in which school officials, employees or agents have been, as a matter of fact, negligent. Negligence consists in having done something which a person ought not have done, or failed to do something which he should have done, out of which the injury arises. There are three vital elements, all three of which must be present for liability to lie:

a. There must be a duty owed the plaintiff by the defendant;
b. There must be a breach of the duty owed; and
c. The breach must constitute the proximate cause of the injury.

Whether defendants have been as a matter of fact negligent is for the jury to determine, on appropriate instructions from the bench. But it is well settled that the school district cannot be held liable for an actionable wrong unless one of its employees has been negligent as a matter of fact. The following case, *Carroll v. Fitzsimmons*, 384 P.2d 81, Colo. 1963, illustrates this point of law.

52   *Immunity of District Officials*

An elementary school student was injured on the playground when hit in the head by a rock thrown by another student at recess. The mother, on behalf of her son and herself, instituted a suit for damages against individual board members, the county superintendent, the district superintendent, the principal and the teacher in charge of the playground at the time of the injury. Claim was made that the teacher was negligent in allowing the rock to be thrown. While the immunity that cloaks a school district under the common law is no shield to school officials, they would be liable only if the teacher was negligent. In this case, the teacher was not the tort feasor, hence the other parties to the suit would not be held liable for damages in connection with the child's injuries.

Relief Sought: Damages for personal injuries received on school playground allegedly because of the negligence of school officials

Issue: Can the school district and the school's officials be held liable for damages for an injury allegedly due to teacher negligence?

Holding of the Trial Court: Complaint dismissed

Holding of the Appellate Court: Affirmed

Reasoning

The facts alleged against the elementary school teacher are not actionable. The school teacher was not the tort feasor. There is no requirement that general supervision be constant and unremitting nor that it be continuous and direct. The other individuals would be held liable, if at all, only under the theory of "respondeat superior." Dismissal of the claim against the teacher disposes of the claims against all of the superiors of the teacher. Instrumentality: A rock is not considered to be a dangerous weapon. Time: The blow was instantaneous, and even had the teacher been standing beside the pupil, she could not have prevented the accident.

Significance

A teacher may not be held liable for student injury in the absence of a statement of claim upon which relief may be granted by the courts. Under the doctrine of respondeat superior, the school board members as individuals, the superintendent and principal may not be held liable unless the teacher has been held liable in negligence. Dismissal of the claim against the teacher disposes of the claim against the superiors of the teacher.

CASE CITATION: *Carroll v. Fitzsimmons, 384 P.2d 81 (Colo. 1963)*

53   Tort Immunity of School Districts

Because of the noise from partition construction work in the regular classroom, the teacher of a metal class took the class outside on the lawn where they sat in a semi-circle facing him. It was review work for a written examination on safety. The teacher would read a question, then glance up occasionally for discussion or questions. Some boys were flipping a homemade knife into the ground. After about thirty minutes, the knife struck a drawing board and bounced upward into the plaintiff's eye. The teacher testified that he did not see the knife before the accident and that his first knowledge that anything was wrong was when he heard the plaintiff's outcry.

Relief Sought: Damages for injury sustained by a student during school hours while under the supervision of a teacher who allegedly acted negligently

Issue: What standard of care is required of the school's employees in the supervision of students?

Holding of the Trial Court: In favor of the defendant school district

Holding of the Appellate Court: Judgment reversed

Reasoning

What is ordinary care depends upon the circumstances of each particular case, and is to be determined as a matter of fact by the jury on instructions from the bench. There was evidence that the knife throwing had been going on for some time before the accident. The teacher should have observed this, and taken action to prevent what in fact happened, an injury to one of the students. Failing to know this, or to stop it in time to prevent the accident amounted to a breach of the duty owed the student by the teacher, since a reasonably prudent person would have had the foresight to see that an accident might occur under those or similar circumstances. There was also a causal link between the teacher's failure to exercise ordinary care and the injury to the student. The judge, in directing the verdict in favor of the school district, was in error and ought to be reversed.

Significance

School teachers must meet the norm of behavior which an ordinarily prudent adult would exercise under the same or similar circumstances. Whether this standard of care has been met will be a question of fact for the jury on appropriate instructions from the bench. The outcome is subject, however, to appeal on error on points of law, but seldom if ever on matters of fact.

CASE CITATION: *Lilienthal v. San Leandro Unified School District, 293 P.2d 889 (Calif. 1956)*

AUTHOR'S COMMENTARY

California is among the states which have abrogated the doctrine of governmental immunity; school districts in that state may be held liable for their tortious acts where employees or school officials have acted in a negligent manner. In the *Lilienthal* case *supra* the district was liable for the damages incurred because of the negligence of the classroom teacher.

Liability of school officials or employees or of the district itself arises because of the "safe place concept," which is that school children, who are at their schools through the insistence of the state's compulsory attendance laws, may be assumed by their natural parents to be in a "safe place" while absent from home. Another California case which arose in 1929 will serve to illustrate this concept. A piano was kept in the high school gymnasium and moved from room to room on a dolly. The piano was not attached to the dolly, but merely rested upon it. About a year after it was mounted on the dolly, the piano toppled over and pinned a girl's ankle to the floor. The court said that school officials should have noticed the possibility of danger and taken steps to prevent injury to the students; in other words, have made sure that the students were in a "safe place." Failure to take note of this defective equipment and take positive steps to prevent accidents resulting from it amounted to negligence, for which the school district was liable. *Dawson v. Tulare Union Dist.,* 276 Pac. 424 (Calif. 1929).

In an immunity state, the situation is somewhat different; since the school district is immune, the employee may be held personally liable for his own negligence. In Kansas, a school custodian burned out a tree stump on the school grounds, but left the fire unextinguished and unguarded. A boy playing on the school grounds stepped into the coals and was severely burned. While protecting the district under the governmental immunity doctrine, the court nonetheless held that a cause of action existed on the part of the boy against the custodian as an employee of the school district. "A public employee," said the court, "should be held accountable for his negligent acts to those who suffer injury by reason of his misconduct, even though he is about the business of his employer, which is immune from tort liability under the governmental immunity doctrine." *Rose v. Board of Education of Abilene,* 337 P.2d 652 (Kans. 1959).

Finally, the "safe place" doctrine extends to failure to act on the part of the teacher. A group of small boys took a teeter board from its upright, and placed it across a swing. The plaintiff, and a number of other boys, placed themselves on the board and began to teeter. Shortly after they began this form of play, the school bell rang, and the boys on the opposite side of the teeter suddenly sprang from it, permitting the side on which the plaintiff sat to rapidly descend, striking him upon the ankle, causing injury. The court said that the teacher was negligent.

> If the teacher knew it (that the boys were using the teeter board in a way contrary to the way it was supposed to be used), it was negligence to permit it, and if she did not know it, it was negligence not to have observed it. If the accident happened in the manner and time as contended, and the teacher was present, then supervision was inadequate and there was negligence in permitting pupils to use the board in this way. *Bruenn v. North Yakima School District,* 172 Pac. 569 (Wash. 1918).

54   *Tort Immunity of School Districts*

The school district conducted a recreational program open to the general public upon payment of an admission fee. The program, which was not part of the regular curriculum, consisted of those activities normal to a summer day camp including arts and crafts, dancing and swimming. Plaintiff's minor decedent, Constance Morris, was duly enrolled in the recreation program upon payment by her parents of the weekly charge. Constance drowned while playing in the waters of the swimming pool. Connie's father contended failure of the district to provide proper supervision, and said that the rough and disorderly play in the water allowed by employees of the school district amounted to negligence for which the school district should be held liable.

Relief Sought: Damages for wrongful death of a child

Issue: Does a quasi-municipal corporation engaged in a summer recreation program enjoy governmental immunity?

Holding of the Trial Court: Dismissed

Holding of the Appellate Court: Reversed and reinstated the complaint with a procedendo (writ directing lower court to give judgment)

Reasoning

School districts may operate a governmental program, which is their appointed function, for which they are protected under the doctrine of governmental immunity. They may also operate a proprietary activity, for which they may be held liable if negligence is present. An act may be designated as proprietary "if it is one which a local government unit is not statutorily required to perform, or if it may also be carried on by private enterprise, or if it is used as a means of raising revenue." The operation of a summer recreation program meets all three of these criteria. It is not required of the school district by law. It is an activity which could just as well be carried out by a private corporation. Finally, it was a means of raising revenue, since persons who took part in it were charged a fee. Charging a fee entitles one to a higher standard of protection than if such a fee were not charged. Therefore, the school district comes under the shadow of operating a proprietary activity, and if the jury finds that there was negligence in the operation of the swimming pool, plaintiff may recover.

Significance

Greater protection from tort liability is available to the board of education while conducting a governmental activity, than while conducting a proprietary activity. The former is required, it is something which the school district can do better than a private firm, and there is no charge for the service. But when a district undertakes to conduct a proprietary activity, it may step outside the protection which the law affords it while conducting a governmental function.

CASE CITATION: *Morris v. School Dist. of the Twp. of Lebanon, 144 A.2d 737 (Pa. 1958)*

AUTHOR'S COMMENTARY

Scarce is the school district of any size today which does not conduct a program of "proprietary" activities over and beyond its governmental function of educating the young. The distinction between a governmental and a proprietary function, although clearly delineated in the *Morris* case *supra,* is not easy for the courts to determine. What were once thought to be luxury activities are now considered "essential," so that the courts must deal with social mores concerning what the society expects of its schools at any given point in time.

In Arizona, a high school student attended a football game between the Ampitheatre High School and the Mesa High School, which was played in the stadium of the Tucson High School. The latter district had leased, for $300, its stadium for the game. The rental was paid by the Ampitheatre High School, and there was an admission charge to get into the game. The complaint charged that the defendant had allowed the railing on the stand to fall into and remain in disrepair, so that it was dangerous, and that the deficiency had obtained for a length of time before the accident. As a result of the negligence of the defendant, plaintiff fell from the grandstand to the ground and sustained serious and painful injuries, causing permanent disablement and heavy medical expenses and loss of wages. His suit was successful. *Sawaya v. Tucson High School Dist.,* 281 P.2d 105 (Ariz. 1955).

The court said that ordinarily the school district, engaged in a governmental activity, cannot be held liable for its negligence, or those of its employees. But when it leases its stadium, the school district is exercising a proprietary function, and is liable for injuries sustained by a spectator who is injured as a result of the district's negligence.

55   *Private and Parochial School Liability*

Pupils were to report to the classroom at 8:30 a. m. On this particular day, all the children were in the room, but the teacher had not yet arrived. When the bell rang at 8:45 for the commencement of classes, the teacher was still absent. About ten minutes later, an incident occurred wherein the plaintiff, a pupil was stabbed in the hand by another boy. There still was no teacher in the classroom. From 8:30 to about 8:45 a. m. most of the boys engaged in horseplay and fighting with one another, and in running and chasing each other about the room. The boy who did the stabbing was seen wielding a knife for some five to ten minutes prior to the actual stabbing. Evidence showed there was a lack of supervision for some 25 minutes prior to the stabbing, which was unprovoked and unwarranted.

Relief Sought: Recovery of damages for injury to a pupil in a parochial school on grounds teacher was negligent

Issue: Is a private or parochial school liable in damages when one of its employees, here a teacher, has been negligent and a pupil is injured?

Holding of the Trial Court: For the plaintiff

Holding of the Appellate Court: Judgment affirmed

Reasoning

Whether the act was done accidentally or intentionally does not matter. What matters is whether a teacher, if present, could have anticipated the act in the reasonable exercise of his duty toward the plaintiff, and whether the teacher could have anticipated the unprovoked attack of the boy on the plaintiff. Had the teacher been present, she would have been able to see, as the members of the class saw, a gradual buildup of excitement, and she would have seen a boy with a dangerous instrument, a six-inch knife, in the hands of one of the students. She would then have been able to have taken proper action to prevent the occurrence which resulted in plaintiff's injury. The stabbing of the plaintiff was an act which reasonably could have been foreseen by the teacher if she were present. Therefore, her absence was the proximate cause of the injury. The stabbing was not an act which could have occurred equally well in the presence of the teacher as during her absence. Therefore, because of the teacher's negligence, the school is liable in damages for insufficient supervision by a member of its staff.

Significance

Private and parochial schools do not enjoy governmental immunity hence may be held liable in damages for the negligent acts of their employees acting in the line of duty. A teacher's absence from the classroom amounts to negligence if an injury occurs to someone under her supervision and her presence would have reasonably prevented the accident. However, if her presence would not have prevented the accident, she cannot be held liable on the grounds of absence alone. (See Case 52, *supra, Carroll v. Fitzsimmons,* for an example of this principle of law.)

CASE CITATION: *Christofides v. Hellenic Eastern Orthodox Christian Church, 227 N.Y.S.2d 946 (1962)*

AUTHOR'S COMMENTARY

When a worshipper tripped over a kneeler permanently extending into the aisle behind the first pew, he brought an action against the church for negligence. *Widell v. Holy Trinity Catholic Church,* 121 N.W.2d 249 (Wisc. 1963). The court refused to throw plaintiff's case out of court on grounds that religion is essential and beneficial to mankind and ought to be encouraged. "The question is," said the court, "whether the benefit to the many should be at the expense of the innocent sufferer of injuries caused by the negligence of an agent of the religious institution in question. When an institution owes a duty of care to another and as a result of carrying on one of its activities whether the enterprise or activity involves financial gain or not and no matter how lofty the purpose or nature, injury to another whether through agents or directly, the breach of duty ought not be excused or justified on the grounds that it is a laudable purpose or one of great public benefit. . . . A religious organization has no immunity simply because it is a religious organization."

However, it is convincingly argued in some cases that so-called "charitable" institutions should be immune from their torts, on the grounds that they have little or no money out of which to pay damages. With the availability of good insurance, however, it is doubtful that the courts will long continue to protect schools or churches even though they "are engaged in a laudable public purpose."

In *Moore v. Order Minor Conventuals,* 164 F.Supp. 711 (N.C. 1958) a church school was not held liable when some boys obtained the key to the chemistry laboratory from Father Dukette and proceeded to make gunpowder, although that was not in the textbook. An explosion permanently injured some of the boys, who brought suit to recover. The court, however, said that a 15-year-old is presumed to have sufficient capacity to be sensitive to danger and to have power to avoid it. The plaintiff who had been previously warned about this possibility, was guilty of contributory negligence and could not collect in damages from the school.

56 Tort Immunity of School Districts

A child was injured in the Mounds View School District in Minnesota. Cause of the injury was defective equipment, in this case a slide in the kindergarten room of an elementary school. Father of the injured pupil brought suit to recover damages, maintaining that the defective slide constituted negligence on the part of the district's employees.

Relief Sought: Damages from the school district for injury to an elementary pupil while in school

Issue: Should the state supreme court overthrow the traditional governmental immunity doctrine and hold a school district liable in negligence?

Holding of the Trial Court: For the school district

Holding of the Minnesota Supreme Court: For the school district, with the understanding that "the defense of sovereign immunity" will thereinafter not be sufficient grounds for school districts avoiding payment of damages

Reasoning

The handwriting has long been on the courtroom wall. We have been troubled for three generations by the unheeded petitions of the lame Frederick Bank, the halt Jennie Snider, and the blind Frank Mokovich (three students hurt at school who could not recover because of the sovereign immunity rule). Since we have repeatedly proclaimed that this defense is based on neither justice nor reason, the time is now at hand when corrective measures should be taken by either legislative or judicial fiat. . . . Some states have already abolished the distinction between governmental and proprietary functions in keeping with the modern tendency which is to restrict rather than extend the doctrine of municipal immunity. The injustice of the immunity doctrine to injured individuals in this era of rapidly expanding governmental functions and service is apparent. We recognize that by denying recovery in the case at bar the remainder of the decision becomes dictum. However, the court is unanimous in expressing its intention to overrule the doctrine of sovereign immunity as a defense with respect to tort claims against school districts. . . . The rule that we are asked to apply is out of tune with the life about us. It has been made discordant by the forces that generate a living law. We apply it to this case because the repeal might work hardship to those who have trusted in its existence. We give notice, however, that any one trusting in it hereafter will do so at his peril.

Significance

What the courts have originally decided, as in *Russell,* they can overthrow at a later date. No one should have to suffer in silence for the actionable wrongs of others, even though they be engaged in a very important function, that of educating the youth of this country. For every wrong there must be a compensating relief available, a piece of justice unavailable to earlier plaintiffs (named) because of the sovereign immunity doctrine.

CASE CITATION: *Spanel v. Mounds View School District, 118 N.W.2d 795 (Minn. 1962)*

AUTHOR'S COMMENTARY

Inasmuch as Minnesota at the time was an "immunity state," the three individuals mentioned in the *Spanel* case were denied recovery for injuries suffered at the hands of a state subdivision. Frederick Bank was an eight-year-old boy who was denied recovery for the loss of a leg due to an accident on school property. The court said that the school district was "purely a public good, for which they receive no private or corporate benefit, and they are not therefore liable to an individual for the negligence of their servants in the business of such agency. *Bank v. Brainerd School District,* 51 N.W. 814 (Minn. 1892).

Jennie Snider's foot was crushed by a city-hall elevator, but she was not permitted to recover. *Snider v. City of St. Paul,* 53 N.W. 763 (Minn. 1892). As for Frank Mokovich, he was blinded by the use of unslaked lime in marking a football field. *Mokovich v. Independent School District No. 22,* 225 N.W. 292 (Minn. 1929).

The Supreme Court of Pennsylvania asserted that waiving the tort immunity rule for school boards is not within the function of the courts. *Supler v. School District,* 182 A.2d 535 (Pa. 1963). Said the court:

> If it is to be the policy of the law that the Commonwealth or any of its instrumentalities or any political subdivisions are to be subject to liability for the torts committed by their officers or employees while engaged in governmental functions, the change should be made by the Legislature and not by the Courts.

However, in *Spanel,* the Supreme Court of Minnesota said, in part:

> We do not share the view that a court-made rule, however unjust or outmoded, becomes with age invulnerable to judicial attack and cannot be discarded except by legislative action. *Spanel v. Mounds View School District,* 118 N.W.2d 799 (Minn. 1962)

Despite this view on the part of the Minnesota court, however, it did not allow recovery on the *Spanel* case, leaving to the legislature the question of to what extent it would go in assessing liability against state subdivisions.

It therefore assured protection for school districts under the doctrine of sovereign immunity until a later date before which the legislature would be able to meet and consider the problem. The legislature, in its next session established a moratorium by reinstating the doctrine for a specified period of time.

57 *Tort Immunity of School Districts*

On March 10, 1958 a school bus of the Kaneland school district left the road, allegedly as the result of the driver's negligence, hit a culvert, exploded and burned. Fourteen children riding in the bus at the time were injured, some permanently because of the accident. A motion to dismiss on immunity basis was granted by the trial court, and plaintiffs appealed. Some six years later, after much litigation, some of it in the U.S. Supreme Court, the court held for plaintiffs in the amount of $875,000. At the time of the accident, the district carried liability insurance of $20,000 for each person injured and $100,000 limit on each accident, far short of the funds needed to pay damages under the court's edict. In 1964, the state turned over to the district a check in the amount of $750,000 to cover the remainder of the claims. Legality of using state funds to reimburse the district was one of the reasons for going to the U.S. Supreme Court.

> *Relief Sought:* Recovery of damages for injuries sustained in a school bus accident

Issue: Should the state supreme court abrogate the doctrine of non-liability of school districts?

Holding of the Trial Court: Dismissed on grounds school district was immune

Holding of the Supreme Court of Illinois: Reversed

Reasoning

Education constitutes one of the nation's biggest businesses. The doctrine started by *Russell* is now obsolete in England, and we have not honored it since 1898 in Illinois. In this day and age, school districts are as capable of satisfying judgments based on the tortious conduct of their servants as any private business. The cost of liability insurance is one of the costs of operating education, and can and should be spread over the district in the same way as other educational expenses. The legislature has authorized school districts to purchase liability insurance, and there is no reason to deny the propriety of spending the funds to pay the liability itself in the absence of insurance. The Revolutionary War was fought to abolish "the divine right of kings" on which the theory (of non-liability of school districts) is based.

Significance

In the words of the court, the doctrine of school district non-liability was created by the courts, and it can and should be abolished by the courts; where it has outlasted its usefulness, the doctrine should be eradicated.

CASE CITATION: *Molitor v. Kaneland Community Unit School District, 163 N.E.2d 89 (Ill. 1959)*

AUTHOR'S COMMENTARY

Of all the cases involving non-liability of school districts for their torts, the *Molitor* case is the best known (John P. Linn, "Tort Liability and the Schools," *N. Dak. Law Review,* Summer 1967, pp. 765–774). It represented a state supreme court's attempts to provide a remedy for those who were injured as a result of school district negligence. Despite this example, "one may discern a persistent effort to negate the immunity doctrine; yet it is a nibbling process. State legislatures move in a halting and hesitating manner away from the immunity concept by authorizing school districts to purchase some indemnity or liability insurance. But there is no frontal assault that will bring about full scale destruction of the immunity walls. Consequently, school districts go about their business, behind their protective walls, secure in the realization that unless social, economic or political pressures produce a gunpowder more destructive than that produced thus far by legal logic there is little to fear." *Id.* at 774.

58   *Tort Immunity of School Districts*

In Mason City, Iowa a district basketball tournament was being held, when some bleachers collapsed injuring some of the spectators who had paid to see the games. Suit was brought against the School District and against the sponsoring organization, the Iowa High School Athletic Association for damages on the grounds that one or both of them were negligent. The trial court sustained defendants' motion for dismissal on immunity grounds and plaintiffs appealed to the Iowa Supreme Court, which by a narrow vote of five to four upheld the sovereign immunity doctrine and refused to hold the school district liable. The court later ruled that the IHSAA did not come under the same immunity protection, and could be held liable for the injuries.

> *Relief Sought:* Recovery of damages for injuries suffered in collapse of bleachers at a basketball game

Issue: If a school district is not liable for injuries sustained at a state basketball tourney, is the state's athletic association?

Holding of the Trial Court: Dismissed

Holding of the Iowa Supreme Court: By a decision of 5–4 upheld immunity of the state

Reasoning

Majority: We have held many times that if the doctrine of governmental immunity is to be changed it should be done by the legislature. The position we have taken accords with that of most courts. . . . We think experience in the few states where the court has attempted to abrogate the immunity doctrine indicates legislative action is a better solution. *Minority:* The whole doctrine of governmental immunity is outmoded and should be abrogated by the court. If a child is injured as a result of negligence at a private or Sunday school recovery may be had, but if at a public school immunity bars recovery. We can see no necessity for insisting on legislative action in a matter which the courts themselves originated. . . . *Judicial consistency loses its virtue when it is degraded by the vice of injustice.* (Emphasis added by the court) . . . . Why should the legislature interfere when we refuse to correct our past mistakes? It is our duty to see that justice is done. "Policy" or any other reason does not justify our inaction.

Significance

As a result of this case, the Iowa Legislature enacted a statute patterned after the Federal Tort Claims Act applicable to the State, but it was ruled to apply only to state government and not to other governmental units. In 1967, the Legislature passed another act waiving immunity for cities, towns, and school districts and establishing a procedure for filing claims. Unlike most other tort liability acts, however, it did not contain any monetary limitations. See *Graham v. Worthington*, 146 N.W.2d 626 (Iowa 1966) and Iowa Senate File 710, Sixty-second General Assembly, Laws of 1967.

CASE CITATION: *Boyer v. Iowa High School Athletic Association, 127 N.W.2d 606 (Iowa 1964); 138 N.W.2d 914 (Iowa 1965)*

AUTHOR'S COMMENTARY

Organizations other than school districts that perform education-like functions frequently attempt to avoid being charged with liability by pleading governmental immunity. In the *Boyer* case, the same court which turned down the plaintiffs when they sought to recover damages from the school district, allowed them to recover from the Iowa High School Athletic Association. *Boyer v. Iowa High School Athletic Association*, 138 N.W.2d 914 (Iowa 1965).

A contrary finding occurred when a federal district court extended the defense of governmental immunity to a state's public school building authority. *Rupe v. State Public School Building Authority*, 245 F.Supp. 726 (Pa. 1965). Said the court:

> The Legislature has spoken unequivocally in specifying the purposes of the authority and setting forth its powers "of constructing, improving, maintaining and operating, public school buildings, and furnishing and equipping the same for use as public schools, as a part of the public school system of the Commonwealth of Pennsylvania under the jurisdiction of the Department of Public Instruction." It is plain that the Authority, as thus constituted, has been woven into the fabric of the Pennsylvania educational system as a governmental function and operated ex officio by the State's executive officers. . . . What the Legislature did was, in effect, to give the Department of Public Instruction another arm in aiding it to administer the public school system of the Commonwealth. It was a proper and constitutional action.

59   *Tort Immunity of School Districts*

A state statute in Montana required that school districts owning and operating their own buses must carry, on each bus operated, automobile bodily injury and liability insurance with limits of not less than $7,500 per person and $50,000 per accident. The board operated within this law, and had the requisite insurance, but defended on the ground of governmental immunity. The trial court held for the board, but the higher court reversed the decision of the trial court. In a lengthy decision, the court dealt with several issues related to governmental immunity of school districts.

Relief Sought: Recovery of damages for injury allegedly at the negligence of the school district's employees

Issue: When a school district is required by statute to carry automobile bodily injury and liability insurance on its school buses, is its governmental immunity from tort liability impliedly waived, at least, to the amounts of such insurance actually or required to be carried by the school district?

Holding of the Trial Court: For defendant board of education

Holding of the Appellate Court: Reversed

Reasoning

Common law: 1) School districts are ordinarily not liable for their torts unless made so by the legislature. 2) Free transportation for pupils to public schools is generally considered a governmental function. 3) *Statutory law:* voluntary procurement of liability insurance does not waive that unit's immunity because the power to waive rests with the legislature. We fail to see how it can be argued that the Legislature would require insurance to be carried and then deny any means of recovery to an individual injured in connection with the operation of a school bus. We do not think the Legislature would simply have meant to enrich insurance companies. This cannot be. . . . We hold that the . . . Legislative Assembly by requiring school districts to carry liability insurance, waived only to the extent of the insurance required or actually carried, the school district's immunity from suit.

Significance

As courts lift the veil of immunity, they recognize that there must still be some protection for the school district. Some districts do not carry insurance beyond that reasonably awarded by the courts. The courts, therefore, have generally held that the veil can be lifted only to the extent of the insurance actually carried by the school district, although the *Molitor* case is a major exception.

CASE CITATION: *Longpre v. Joint School District No. 2, 443 P.2d 1 (Mont. 1968)*

AUTHOR'S COMMENTARY

In *Supler v. School District,* 182 A.2d 535 (Pa. 1962) the court said that abrogation of the tort immunity doctrine for school districts must come from the legislature. The school district receives no value for its money, said the plaintiffs, if it purchases liability insurance, then receives no protection from it. The fallacy in this argument, returned the court, is that insurance protects the school district against liability in performing *proprietary* functions, and it needs no protection in performing its governmental functions, since it is immune. With respect to whether the presence of insurance allows recovery, it would seem to be unjust to allow recovery to an injured person where an authority is not insured. The right to recovery would then depend not upon the principles of justice and the magnitude of the injury but upon whether insurance was carried and if so, to what amount.

In *Benedetto v. Travelers Insurance Company,* 172 So.2d 354 (La. 1965) the court would not allow recovery where a girl of 12 or 13 was sitting in such a position as to be struck by a bat in a softball game. "Baseball (softball) is well known to all," said the court. "Cheryl was aware of the possible danger (in sitting where she did), so was guilty of contributory negligence." The suit was brought against the insuror on the grounds that playground supervision was inadequate and the school district was liable, but the court could not agree.

Similarly, in another Louisiana case, a child was crushed under the wheels of a bus at the bus loading center when he stooped over to pick up a book as the bus came to a slow halt. The driver had previously warned the children about coming into the street to be picked up. The court found no negligence on the part of the driver. *Norris v. American Casualty Company,* 176 So.2d 677 (La. 1965). There can be no liability in the absence of any negligence. *Landry v. Travelers Indemnity Co.,* 155 So.2d 102; *Oxner v. Reeves,* 153 S.2d 565.

A North Carolina court denied recovery to a plaintiff who took approximately one tablespoon of sodium peroxide from an unlocked cabinet in the classroom. A high school teacher was not in the room at the time the plaintiff took the chemical from the cabinet. The boy knew that the chemical would burn when exposed to water. He became engaged in play, became sweaty, and placed his hand in his pocket to withdraw the chemical, when it exploded. He sustained severe burns and permanent and serious disfigurement. In his suit for damages, he maintained that the school district should have to pay, despite the fact that it had not taken out liability insurance, a practice permitted by the state.

The court ruled in favor of the board. *McBride v. North Carolina State Board of Education,* 125 S.E.2d 393 (N.C. 1962). "Employees of city and county administrative units have governmental immunity," said the court. "These city and county administrative units may by taking liability insurance waive their governmental immunity and hence be held liable for the torts of their employees. But the Guilford County Board of Education did not take out liability insurance. A claim of recovery cannot be brought against a county board of education which has not taken out liability insurance."

60 *Liability for Improper Supervision*

Plaintiff, then aged 13 and a pupil in a drawing class in PS-238 in Brooklyn was severely injured when struck in the eye by a pencil thrown by another pupil. The teacher was absent from the classroom at the time down the hall storing instructional materials in a closet. The length of time teacher was absent from the room was in doubt, but it was lengthy. Plaintiff sought damages from the school district which in New York may be held liable for the tortious acts of its employees.

Relief Sought: Damages for personal injuries suffered by plaintiff, then a pupil in the public schools allegedly because of the teacher's absence from the classroom

Issue: Should the court hold the school board liable for negligence of a teacher who absents herself from the classroom and injuries occur to student?

Holding of the Trial Court: For plaintiff

Holding of the Appellate Court: Reversed

Reasoning

Whether tossing the pencil was done mischievously and heedlessly or wantonly and willfully, or with the serious purpose of returning the pencil to its owner, it was the act of an intervening third party which under the circumstances could hardly have been anticipated in the reasonable exercise of the teacher's legal duty toward the plaintiff. . . . A teacher may be charged only with reasonable care such as a parent of ordinary prudence would exercise under comparable circumstances. 1) *Instrumentality:* No one can seriously contend that a pencil in the hands of a school pupil is a dangerous instrumentality. 2) *Time element:* This is one of those events which could occur equally as well in the presence of the teacher as during her absence, since . . . it was instantaneous, and did not build. The teacher was not negligent in leaving the room, since her presence would not assure that no child would be injured. Therefore it does not follow that the board is liable for an unforeseen act of a third party.

Significance

The teacher's absence from the room will not constitute negligence unless her presence would have prevented the accident from happening. See Case No. 55, *supra Christofides v. Hellenic Eastern Orthodox Christian Church of New York,* 227 N.Y.S.2d 946 (N.Y. 1962).

Case Citation: *Ohman v. Board of Education of City of New York, 90 N.E.2d 474 (N.Y. 1949)*

61   *Standard of Care*

In the regular course of prescribed classes the students in an elementary school had an adjoining classroom for plants and pets. Various students were asked to water and feed these plants and animals to acquaint them with the subject studied. Some of the plants were hanging from the ceiling by wire because of the lack of space. The teacher asked the plaintiff, Elizabeth Gaincott, then eight years of age, to water the plants in the adjoining room. The defendant knew the plaintiff would use a glass milk bottle for the water. She also knew that plaintiff could not reach the higher plants without extra support. With the defendant's permission, the girl used a chair to gain additional height. While on the chair, Elizabeth dropped the glass bottle which broke on the floor. At almost the same instant, she fell from the chair onto the broken glass and severely lacerated her left wrist. She was permanently injured, and brought suit against the teacher alleging negligence.

Relief Sought: Damages for personal injuries

Issue: Was the defendant negligent in allowing an eight year old girl to perform hazardous duties in the classroom?

Holding of the Trial Court: For defendant teacher

Holding of the Appellate Court: Affirmed

Reasoning

There was nothing in the nature of the act itself or the instrumentalities with which plaintiff was permitted to perform the act which would lead a reasonably careful and prudent person to anticipate that the child's safety or welfare were endangered in the performance of the act. The mere fact that an accident occurred, and one that was unfortunate, does not render defendant liable. The commission of watering plants and feeding animals had been one of the class activities. Other students had carried out their duties many times without injuries, and there was no reason for the defendant to suspect that it could not be done again in equal safety. A teacher must possess only average foreseeability, and the teacher cannot be the insuror of the pupil's safety at all times and under every circumstance. All that is expected is that she shall possess that foresight which the normally prudent parent would possess under the same or similar circumstances.

Significance

The foreseeability of the teacher must be only that which the normal adult of average ability might display under the same or similar circumstances.

CASE CITATION: *Gaincott v. Davis, 275 N.W. 229 (Mich. 1937)*

62 Standard of Care

Defendant Stanford was a physical education instructor. He ordered two students to box three rounds of one minute each. The students were vigorous and strong, but untrained in the art of self-defense. The defendant watched from the bleachers. In the second round, the plaintiff was hit in the temple and became dizzy. A prolonged headache followed, and he then lost consciousness. Subsequently, a doctor diagnosed the trouble as a cerebral hemorrhage, and several operations were necessary. Plaintiff described the contest as vigorous, ending with a blow to his temple in the second round. No contrary evidence was presented.

Relief Sought: Damages from teacher who was allegedly negligent

Issue: Is the teacher who allows pupils to engage in hazardous exercise without proper training negligent, hence liable, if an injury occurs to one of the pupils?

Holding of the Trial Court: For the plaintiff

Holding of the Court of Appeals: Judgment affirmed, with costs

Reasoning

It is a teacher's duty to exercise reasonable care towards those under his tutelage or supervision. In ordering or permitting two young men to enter into a match of this kind without defensive training or warning of the danger was negligence. The teacher failed in his duty and was therefore liable. Students should be warned before being permitted to engage in hazardous activities. The teacher failed to warn the plaintiff and he is entitled to recover.

Significance

The standard of care of the teacher toward his pupils is that he must tell them if there are any "known hazards" involved, and instruct them in self-defense or otherwise assure that they are protected from harm. 1) If there is a duty owed; 2) If there is a breach of the duty; 3) And if the breach is the proximate cause of the injury, defendant is negligent and the plaintiff may recover.

CASE CITATION: *Lavalley v. Stanford, 70 N.Y.S.2d 460 (N.Y. 1947)*

AUTHOR'S COMMENTARY

The question of whether an injury to a pupil is foreseeable, hence avoidable, has often been before the courts. Whether the teacher's actions are the "proximate cause" of the injury is a matter of fact for the jury. A Minnesota case will illustrate.

Diane, a second grader, was under the supervision of her physical education teacher, Miss Williams. She was jumping rope as a part of the regular curriculum of this class. The rope used was 6 feet long and had wooden handles on each end. Each pupil was permitted to continue jumping until either the rope was stepped upon by the jumper, or was stopped as the result of striking the jumper's foot. At the time Diane was jumping, the rope was held by a classmate and the defendant. Diane's feet came down on the rope as it was being rotated, so that the wooden handle was pulled from the teacher's grasp and flew toward Diane, striking one of her upper front teeth. Her parents brought suit for damages.

In denying damages, the court said that the rope (instrumentality) was the same as those ordinarily used by children for many years. The teacher could not have anticipated that because the rope was no longer than 6 feet, or because it was equipped with wooden handles, that it would be jerked out of her grasp, resulting in an injury to the girl. Circumstances always determine negligence; where there is no negligence, as here, the incapabilities of the injured child do not of themselves create a liability. *Wire v. Williams,* 133 N.W.2d 840 (Minn. 1965).

63   *Standard of Care*

A high school letter club planned an initiation ceremony for which the athletic coach obtained permission of the superintendent of schools to use the high school gymnasium. Initiates were administered an electric shock by means of a home-made device plugged into an outlet in the school building. The apparatus consisted of a crude rheostat made from a jar of distilled water in which a quantity of salt had been dissolved. Several wires were placed on the gym floor and each initiate had to assume a prostrate position across the wires while balancing a container of water on his chest. The fourth boy subjected to this trick lay on a wet floor, for some of the water spilled from the container. He was electrocuted and died almost instantly.

Relief Sought: Damages for wrongful death of a son in a school activity

Issue: Is a superintendent held liable for damages when he has assigned one of his staff to supervise an activity and death to one of the students results?

Holding of the Trial Court: For plaintiff; both superintendent and coach were held liable

Holding of the Appellate Court: Superintendent not held liable; coach was

Reasoning

The coach said that he had no official jurisdiction or supervision over the club members during the initiation, but that he had tested the device and found it satisfactory. The facts disclose, said the court, that the coach actively participated in the initiation ceremonies, that it was he who tested the electrical appliance, and that he played an active part in this whole procedure of administering the electric shock. We are of the opinion, therefore, that so far as his liability is concerned, it is immaterial whether he was acting in a personal capacity or in his capacity as athletic coach or teacher. As for the superintendent, his duty owed the plaintiff, if any, was dispatched through appointment of a member of the staff, the coach, to be present at the activity, and he cannot be held to have been negligent in so doing.

Significance

The employee directly in charge of the activity in which a student is injured is the one liable when negligence is present. The superintendent, on the other hand, discharges his duty to the student by appointing someone from the faculty or other adult to be present at the event.

CASE CITATION: *Degooyer v. Harkness, 13 N.W.2d 815 (S.D. 1944)*

AUTHOR'S COMMENTARY

In Washington, where school districts are made liable for certain torts, the Supreme Court of that state held a school district liable in damages in an action brought by a boy who was injured while being initiated into Key Club, an organization sponsored by the Kiwanis Club. *Chappell v. Franklin Pierce School District,* 426 P.2d 471 (Wash. 1967). The board denied responsibility since the initiation was held outside school hours and off school property. There was a school sponsor for this club, and for some reason it met off campus, although there was a school rule that forbade this practice. In the light of these facts, the court held the board liable.

> Where, as here, the evidence reveals that educational and cultural values inhere in the normal activities of an extracurricular student body organization, and the school administration has assumed supervisory responsibility over the organization which, in turn, extends to tacit approval of and faculty participation in planning and supervising off-campus initiation ceremonies involving physical ordeal, the school district cannot relieve itself of potential tort liability arising out of an initiation stunt upon the grounds that, standing alone, the initiation rite possesses no educational or cultural value.

However, the same court held the Seattle school district liable for the wrongful death of a student who was crushed to death when sheets of plywood toppled, pinning his body against the wall. The question for the jury was whether the wood was stored safely. The lower court ruled against the board, and on appeal was upheld by the Supreme Court of Washington. *Swartley v. Seattle School District,* 421 P.2d 1009 (Wash. 1967).

64   *School as a "Safe Place"*

Plaintiff, 14 years old, was in a gym class together with 48 other boys. Mr. Sherry, the coach and instructor, told them to shoot baskets, and left the gymnasium. The boys became rowdy, resulting in plaintiff's being knocked to the floor, where he sustained multiple injuries. His parents brought suit against the school district and the teacher, contending that negligence of the teacher was the proximate cause of the boy's injuries. The school defended by saying that 1) Donald's rowdiness contributed to his injuries; 2) the teacher breached no duty to plaintiff; and 3) the school is not the absolute insuror of the student's safety.

Relief Sought: Damages for personal injury to a pupil

Issue: Does a teacher's absence from the classroom or gymnasium constitute negligence when pupil injury occurs?

Holding of the Trial Court: For Defendant City of Milwaukee

Holding of the Appellate Court: Reversed

Reasoning

In the instant case it cannot be held as a matter of law that the rowdyism of the participants in the keep-away game was a superseding cause of plaintiff's injury. If, under the circumstances, defendant's absence from the classroom is negligence, the fact that the boy's conduct or that of the other participants in the game was also a substantial factor does not excuse Sherry (the teacher). A jury could find that the teacher acted unreasonably in leaving a class of almost 50 adolescent boys unsupervised for 25 minutes. This is a breach of his duty to the student. Also, it is definitely up to the jury to decide the degree of contributory negligence on the part of the student. Even though a teacher may leave a class unsupervised, he may not do so for an unreasonable length of time, especially when the circumstances are such that injury is a likelihood, as in free play.

Significance

If a teacher's presence would have prevented an accident to a student, his absence is the proximate cause of the injury even though the student is big enough to know that injury might result where the circumstances indicate this possibility. While the teacher is neither immune from liability nor is he an "insuror" of his students' safety, he is still liable for injuries resulting from his failure to exercise reasonable care. To permit a recovery where the defendant is found to be negligent is not to render that defendant an insuror.

CASE CITATION: *Cirillo v. City of Milwaukee, 150 N.W.2d 460 (Wisc. 1967)*

65 *Standard of Care*

Plaintiff, a grandmother, was invited to attend a football game in which her grandson was to play. Admission was free because it was a third team playing. She was standing with her back to the game near the fifty yard line conversing with her daughter when a player who was carrying the ball was tackled and knocked out of bounds. The grandmother was injured and brought suit to recover damages, claiming that the school district officials were negligent for failing to keep spectators back from the sidelines. The trial court dismissed her case and she appealed.

Relief Sought: Damages by a spectator who was injured at a school football game

Issue: Does a spectator assume some risk when attending a school athletic event?

Holding of the Trial Court: Dismissed

Holding of the Washington Supreme Court: Affirmed

Reasoning

It is argued that there could be no assumption of risk as the plaintiff had no knowledge of the game of football and could not assume a risk of which she had no knowledge. While it is clear that a plaintiff must know the risk before it can be assumed, it is equally clear that he cannot deny knowledge of the obvious. Had plaintiff been watching the game for the fifteen seconds prior to the time she was hit, she would have seen an end run developing and coming in her direction, and she could doubtless have gotten out of the way as everyone else did. However, she was not watching the game, but was engaging in a conversation with a friend; and she did not see the approaching ball carrier until he was too close for her to avoid him. Even conceding the ignorance of the game claimed, some objective standard of negligence must be applied. She cannot be heard to say that she did not comprehend a risk which would be apparent to a reasonably prudent and cautious person. The plaintiff had a duty to protect herself not only against dangers of which she had actual knowledge, but such dangers incident to the game as would be apparent to a reasonable person in the exercise of due care.

Significance

A spectator at a school game assumes some risk in attending, and cannot be heard to complain where his actions have contributed to his injury.

CASE CITATION: *Perry v. Seattle School District, 405 P.2d 589 (Wash. 1966)*

AUTHOR'S COMMENTARY

In Louisiana, a case with a similar factual situation arose. The case also involved a grandmother who went to see her grandson play football. The question of district immunity was not raised. The trial court held for the defendant school board and plaintiff appealed. No accommodations were provided for the spectators, who numbered some 1,500 or 2,000 strong, and no attempt was made to control the crowd. The issues were 1) was the plaintiff an invitee? and 2) did she assume a risk in attending the game which would bar recovery?

A higher degree of care is owed an invitee than a licensee. Plaintiff claimed her status was that of an invitee, since the game was advertised in the newspapers, and was sponsored by school officials. The court held she was indeed at least an implied invitee. The grandmother asserted she had never attended a football game and had no actual knowledge of the rules or customs of the game, but the court rejected her claim. *Turner v. Caddo Parish School Board,* 179 So.2d 702 (La. 1966).

These cases are in harmony with earlier cases involving injuries to spectators. "Any person of ordinary intelligence cannot watch a game of hockey for any length of time without realizing the risks involved to players and spectators alike," said one court in denying recovery to a spectator injured at a hockey game. *Modec v. City of Eveleth,* 29 N.W.2d 453 (Minn. 1947). Similarly, no one can claim ignorance of the risk from flying foul balls at a baseball game. *Brisson v. Minneapolis Baseball & Athletic Ass'n.,* 240 N.W. 903 (Minn. 1932). See also Nolte, "Spectator Assumes Legal Risk," *American School Board Journal,* Aug. 1966, pp. 42–3.

66   *Assumption of Risk*

Plaintiff when a freshman of 15 years of age in the Nyassa High School registered for football and met the requirements, which were that he was physically fit according to a physician and had the written consent of his parents. On October 9, he suffered a permanent neck injury when tackled during a football game. When he reached 21, plaintiff brought action alleging that at the time of his injury he was inexperienced and weighed only 140 pounds, that he was not physically coordinated, and that the equipment and training he received were inadequate. He had been on the junior high school team and played the same position, had been tackled many times, and evidence showed he had received instruction in practice.

Relief Sought: Damages for a permanent injury suffered by a football player

Issue: Can the district and/or its employees be held liable for an injury suffered during a regularly scheduled football game, or does the player assume a risk in going out for the sport?

Holding of the Trial Court: Awarded damages in the amount of $25,000

Holding of the Appellate Court: Reversed

Reasoning

Both teams were well matched. There were some big boys on both teams so this was no cause for claiming that the opposing team contained big, rough boys. Anyone who knows the game of football must realize that it is a contact sport.

There is no other way to play it. The fact that participants may sustain injury is self-evident. Therefore, a football player assumes some risk by going out for the sport. Proper precautions were taken by the coach to assure that the boys would be able to fend for themselves in a game. The tackle in question was made according to the rules and fairly. Plaintiff used his head as a "battering ram" and in so doing should have known that he could sustain a neck injury.

Significance

Athletic coaches must exercise reasonable care for the protection and safety of their players. When injury occurs, in the absence of negligence, assumption of risk is a valid defense.

CASE CITATION: *Vendrell v. School District No. 26C, Malheur County, 376 P.2d 406 (Ore. 1962)*

67   The School as a "Safe Place"

Lesley, a 17 year old high school student, was working voluntarily after school hours at the Calhoun High School on stage scenery. She and four other students were on the stage of the auditorium, when the lights suddenly went out, plunging the whole auditorium in darkness. Plaintiff fell into an open hatchway in the stage floor, resulting in personal injuries. Her parents brought suit to recover damages on the grounds that the school district was negligent for 1) failure to have a teacher present (breach of duty) and 2) allowing a dangerous situation to exist in the building.

Relief Sought: Damages for alleged negligence on the part of the district

Issue: Can the school district be held liable for personal injury incurred in a voluntary, unsupervised, after-school activity?

Holding of the Trial Court: For plaintiffs

Holding of the Appellate Court: Reversed

Reasoning

The student in this case contributed at least 50% to the negligence "by running around in the darkened auditorium rather than walking out the clearly marked safe exit." The school could not reasonably foresee that the lights would go out, lacking prior notice. High school pupils do not have to be supervised while working voluntarily on a project such as this one. While the law assumes that children are in a "safe place" it would be unreasonable so to hold a school responsible for all the hazards in a building considered to be safe, especially when the hazard is unforeseeable.

Significance

One defense against a charge of negligence is contributory negligence, i.e., the injured party brings it on himself by his action or lack of foresight. It is not a breach of the duty owed the student not to have a teacher in continual attendance where the project is voluntary and the students are big enough to know and recognize potential dangers.

CASE CITATION: *Tannenbaum v. Board of Education, 255 N.Y.S.2d 522 (N.Y. 1964)*

AUTHOR'S COMMENTARY

Suits for damages will continue because 1) people are "sue conscious"; 2) schools are big business, inviting injury in many places; and 3) the availability of insurance and the gradual disappearance of the tort immunity doctrine from the scene will encourage such litigation. Defenses against suits for damages available to the school district and its staff include a) assumption of risk, b) contributory negligence, c) comparative negligence, in which the liability is pro-rated, and d) the tort immunity doctrine. A school district is more likely to be held to account for its proprietary than for its governmental miscues, but there is a trend to hold school districts liable for their governmental torts as well. As this scene changes, one need but read the cases involving school injuries to realize that teachers, administrators, and school board members have their hands full in trying to provide a "safe place" for children to attend school.

Negligence arises out of a duty owed, a breach of that duty, out of which grows the injury complained of. No person or school district can be held to account in damages where negligence is lacking. The standard of care is that which an average individual with ordinary prudence and foresight would have displayed under the same or similar circumstances. What these are is a matter of fact for the jury to determine.

PART FIVE

School Board Powers
and Duties

Part Five

School Board Powers
and Duties

In a federal union such as that under which Americans live, the powers of government are divided. Since in the nature of things sovereignty cannot be anything but unitary, the powers of various levels of government are brought to bear on this problem or that, depending upon the problem. This is the essence of the federal system—that certain jurisdictions have control over this area while others have control over other areas. Thus, federal, state and municipal and county governments share in the "governing" process; where there is doubt about which level of government shall prevail, the "supremacy" of the Constitution is recognized.

The federal government possesses no inherent powers; what powers it may have are delegated to it by the Constitution of the United States, or are enumerated in the public laws of Congress or spelled out in the Constitution. Since the Constitution is silent on the question of education, the power to regulate a system of free public education is reserved by the Tenth Amendment to the respective states:

> The powers not delegated to the United States by the Constitution, nor prohibited by it to the States, are reserved to the States respectively, or to the people.

The power of the State over education is in turn exercised through its legislative assembly, which is said to have plenary (complete) power over the state's educational system. The legislative bodies in turn have provided for the operation of the schools through the creation of school districts, each of which has a governing local board of education.

Recent experience in which local boards of education have been unable to solve their mounting problems attests to the growth in responsibility given to local boards in solving educational problems and the declining level of power available to the board to solve these problems. Several reasons exist for this erosion of local board powers. The drive to strengthen state boards of education took over some of the local board's powers. Bargaining with teachers' organizations further deprived the board of the right to have the last word. Voluntary membership in regional accreditation and state athletic associations limits board powers, as do statutes enacted by the legislature which tend to centralize power in that body's hands. Other constraints include unrealistic upper bond levy limits, and the rate of interest the districts are allowed to pay on their bonds. Powerful taxpayer and/or parents' groups may further limit the local board of education's powers.

By far the greatest amount of board power has been eroded, however, by the courts, particularly those which deal with the question of whether those with whom the board deals are being accorded their full constitutional rights. Thus, boards may not dismiss teachers for union activity (see Case No. 36), nor enforce rules which deprive the student of basic fundamental rights under the Constitution (see Cases No. 8, 11, 14, 21, and 46).

This section of the present volume is concerned with the enforceable powers of boards of education from the viewpoint of the courts. These seventeen cases illustrate what local boards can and cannot do in the operation of the schools of the district. The briefs reveal far more than a mere perusal of the school codes of the various states would reveal, for when one reads the statute, one is never fully sure of its meaning until it has been tested in a court of law.

68   *Third Parties Dealing with the Board of Education*

This action was instituted to restrain a school board from using any part of the funds raised by a bond issue for the purchase of a school site which did not adjoin a site already in the possession of the school board. Plaintiff contended that an understanding existed between the school board and the electors of the district that, if the issuance of the bonds was approved, a site would be obtained adjacent to one already used for school purposes, and a building would be erected thereon. The court held that the issue was whether an "understanding" with the board was binding on the board. The lower court held it was not, and the court of appeals affirmed the lower court's decision.

Relief Sought: Injunction to prevent the board of education from proceeding with the purchase of school sites other than those adjoining the existing school site of the district

Issue: Can an informal "understanding" exist between the electors and the school board?

Holding of the Trial Court: For defendant school board

Holding of the Appellate Court: Affirmed

Reasoning

Plaintiff contends an understanding is binding on the board. The proposition is not worthy of serious consideration. The law makes no provision for informal understandings of this character. On the contrary, the authorities cited by plaintiff expressly hold that the proposition submitted to the voters, and upon which bonds were voted, and which is later evidenced by the bonds themselves, constitutes a contract, and necessarily the only contract between the parties. In addition, the electors may consult with the school board on the location of the site. But there is no place in the entire procedure for understandings, except such as are expressed in the submission upon which the electors vote. It is nowhere alleged that the site to be purchased was more definitely designated than "for the purchase of school lots" and this without doubt was a sufficient description to present the proposition to the voters.

Significance

Those who deal with the school board do so at their own peril. Those to whom promises or commitments are made are presumed to know that the board is merely giving expression to its present intent, and that it may later change its policy. Where there is no vested interest involved, a promise to do or not to do something is not binding on the board of education.

CASE CITATION: *Jennings v. Clearwater School District, 223 Pac. 84 (Calif. 1924)*

AUTHOR'S COMMENTARY

Third parties unacquainted with the powers of the local school board are often surprised to learn that the board is not bound by a promise, although made in good faith and in full anticipation that the promise will indeed be carried out. What they may fail to realize is that the board is a discretionary body, and has the right to determine at any particular point in time what may be the best course to follow in a particular circumstance. The courts have learned this, and will not interfere in the board's reasonable decisions, unless there is evidence that the board has acted outside its usual powers, or that it acted in an arbitrary, capricious or irresponsible manner.

In Texas, *quo warranto* proceedings were instituted challenging a "promise" the board allegedly made to maintain a certain elementary school even though the district became consolidated. *State v. School District,* 141 S.W.2d 438 (Tex. 1940). It was alleged that after maintaining the elementary school in question for a short while, the board abandoned it, contrary to a pre-election agreement to maintain the school. The court said that the pre-election agreement "was not a contract. . . . Persons acting upon such an agreement were, as a matter of law, we think, charged with notice that the powers of the trustees were conferred by law for public purposes and the exercise thereof, involving, as it does, a matter of future policy, are properly subject to change to meet changing conditions, and could not be restricted by an agreement of the nature of the one here involved." Other cases are to the same effect. *Black v. Strength,* 246 S.W. 79, for example, contains this significant statement: "The board was not binding itself to a certain course of action in the future."

69   *Board Members' Contractual Relationship to the Board*

The Kentucky Attorney-General sought to have a school board member removed from office as a usurper in violation of a state statute which provided that the office of school board member "shall without further action be vacant" if such "member is directly or indirectly interested in the sale of materials to the school district for which school funds are expended." Defendant was a member of a school board, and as sales manager of a bottling company, placed vending machines in the schools. Good business practices were followed and the money profits from the sales were variously used to pay for athletic equipment, lime, paint, fencing, paper, library books, repairs to band instruments, and other school uses. The question turned on whether such funds were "school funds" within the meaning of the statute.

Relief Sought: Removal from the position of board member as a usurper in violation of a state statute

Issue: Does a board member who has an interest in a bottling company vacate his office on the board of education when he sells soft drinks to the school district?

Holding of the Trial Court: For the defendant school board member

Holding of the Appellate Court: Judgment reversed

Reasoning

While the statutes (removing school board members from office) in their operation seem severe, they were not intended to punish members of boards of education, and perhaps in some cases work undeserved hardships upon members when the acts condemned were prompted by no improper motives. There is, however, no distinction made, and none can be made, between the different character of transactions. We are not justified in the inquiry whether these acts were profitable to the members or otherwise. The statutes prohibit the act. These members are guilty of no acts involving even a semblance of moral turpitude. They have merely transgressed the provisions of a statute, perhaps inadvertently. They must, however, suffer the penalties. These statutes were enacted as safeguards upon the spending of public funds and with the further view of throwing a wall of protection around members of such bodies. Their duties as members could not thereby be influenced by selfish interests. The wisdom of such statutes is too apparent to need lengthy discussion.

Significance

School board members, as individuals, should avoid "the very appearance of evil" in their relationships with the board of education. Some states have statutes expressly prohibiting contractual arrangements between individual board members and the board. The wise board member will not place himself or his board in a compromising position in this regard even though his motives may be of the purest and best. When in doubt, the board should steer clear of contractual arrangements of this kind, and in so doing "avoid the very appearance of evil."

CASE CITATION: *Commonwealth of Kentucky ex rel. Breckinridge v. Collins, 379 S.W.2d 436 (Ky. 1964)*

AUTHOR'S COMMENTARY

In states with prohibitory statutes, contracts between the board and one of its members are unenforceable before the law, and the district will not be held to performance of its part of the bargain should litigation result. Such contracts are void on the grounds that "the law never implies an obligation to do that which it forbids the parties to do."

In states having no prohibition against such contracts, it still is unwise although not illegal for a board to enter into a contract with its individual members. Such contracts are merely voidable, not void, and may be ratified and binding on the parties through resolution. *Trainer v. Wolfe,* 21 Atl. 391 (Pa. 1891). Or they may become effective through the actions of the parties, and result in an implied contract. *Smith v. Dandridge,* 135 S.W. 800 (Ark. 1911). If the parties act as if the contract is indeed valid, and both perform under the terms thereof, as if it were so, they in effect create a new contract (implied contract) by their actions.

A school director was employed by the board to supervise construction of a schoolhouse. He performed the work, but was enjoined from cashing his warrant proffered by the board for his services. The court upheld payment of the warrant on the grounds that the courts will not permit the district to receive the property or services of its officers, and then refuse to pay them fairly and reasonably. An implied contract had in fact been created, and the board must be made to pay. *Id.*

In any event, best practice dictates that the board avoid the pitfalls inherent in the practice of contracting with its own individual members. Though intentions may be of the best, there is a place "paved" with such, and exposure will only lead to misunderstanding and discord. It is best when in doubt "to avoid the very appearance of evil" in relations between the body corporate and its individual members.

70   *Removal from Office of School Board Members*

Plaintiff was a teacher seeking to force a ballot synopsis of charges against board members for their recall. The trial court issued the writ prayed for, and the board appealed. The supreme court held that the demand for recall was sufficient to charge the school board members with malfeasance or misfeasance and with violation of their oaths of office, and affirmed the judgment of the lower court. Plaintiff contended the board "conspired" together against her when she requested a hearing following their refusal to re-employ her, and that such a conspiracy amounted to a violation of their oaths of office. She contended also that the board published statements that the Washington Education Association was not impartial; that they were a pressure group; that they had prejudged the subject matter of the pending investigation of personnel relations in the district; and that they were injecting themselves in an obvious attempt either to interfere with or assume the lawful functions of the school board and the court, and further referring to and describing the pending investigation as a "witch hunt."

Relief Sought: Mandamus to compel the designated officer to prepare a ballot synopsis of charges for a recall of the school directors

Issue: Is failure to renew a teacher's contract such a conspiracy as to amount to misfeasance and malfeasance sufficient to provide grounds for a recall ballot?

Holding of the Trial Court: For plaintiffs

Holding of the Appellate Court: Judgment affirmed

Reasoning

We have no constitutional or statutory definition of the words malfeasance or misfeasance. In the cases cited concerning the recall of certain councilmen, the allegation was that certain councilmen agreed to trade votes on certain matters. This court held that such trading did not constitute malfeasance or misfeasance. The courts will not lend their support to an act which tends to corrupt or contaminate, by improper and sinister influences, the integrity of our social or political institutions. Public officers should act from high consideration of public duty, and hence every agreement whose tendency or object is to sully the purity or mislead the judgments of those to whom the high trust is confided is condemned by the courts. The officer may be an executive, administrative, legislative, or judicial officer. The principle is the same in either case.

Significance

The public may expect that their duly elected officers, acting within the scope of their authority, will use their best judgment in handing down their decisions. When they fail to do so, they may be recalled by the electorate provided the state statutes permit such a procedure.

CASE CITATION: *Skidmore v. Fuller, 370 P.2d 975 (Wash. 1962)*

71   Membership in Voluntary Athletic Associations

A high school student filed this complaint against the IHSA, a voluntary association to which his high school belonged. He sought to prevent them from declaring him ineligible to compete in interscholastic competition after December 10, 1962. The trial court held for the plaintiff and the Association appealed. The appellate court reversed the trial court's holding.

Relief Sought: Order restraining the Association from declaring him ineligible to compete in high school athletics

Issue: Can a state athletic association enforce its rules of eligibility without interference from the courts?

Holding of the Trial Court: For plaintiffs

Holding of the Appellate Court: Reversed

Reasoning

The trial court's statement that the evidence demonstrates that there is much uncertainty even as to the year of plaintiff's birth finds abundant support in the record. The Association held three hearings, and on the evidence, held plaintiff ineligible because he had passed his 19th birthday before December 11, 1962. The decisions of any kind of voluntary society or association in disciplining, suspending, or expelling members are of a quasi-judicial character. In such cases, the courts never interfere except to ascertain whether or not the proceedings were pursuant to the rules and laws of the society, whether or not the proceeding was in good faith, and whether or not there was anything in the proceeding in violation of the laws of the land. In the absence of any fraud or collusion, or evidence that the defendants acted unreasonably, arbitrarily, or capriciously, the Athletic Association must be, under the authorities cited, permitted to enforce its rules and orders without interference by the courts.

Significance

A voluntary organization, such as a state athletic association, is entitled to enforce its reasonable rules, and the courts will not interfere with this right, unless there is evidence of fraud, or unreasonable conduct on the part of the association. A board, by becoming a member of such a voluntary association, agrees either by expressed stipulation or by implication, to abide by all rules and regulations of the organization.

CASE CITATION: *Robinson v. Illinois High School Association, 195 N.E.2d 38 (Ill. 1963)*

AUTHOR'S COMMENTARY

The law is well settled that the courts will not take cognizance of a case arising from the expulsion of a member of a voluntary association unless some civil or contractual right is involved. In the internal affairs of a voluntary association, courts do not intervene unless there is a showing of mistake, fraud, collusion or arbitrariness in the proceedings. The reason for this attitude is obvious. The constitution and by-laws of a voluntary association when subscribed or assented to by the members become a contract between each member and the association and if they so provide a member may be expelled for insubordination to the association. *Sult v. Gilbert,* 3 So.2d 729 (Fla. 1941).

At issue in an Indiana case was whether the right to vote in a union election was a civil or property right. The court held that membership in an unincorporated voluntary association is "a privilege and is neither a civil nor a property right." *State ex rel. Givens v. Superior Court of Marion County,* 117 N.E.2d 553 (Ind. 1954).

In Oklahoma, a high school student violated a fixed rule of the state high school athletic association in accepting a gold football. The association ruled the youth ineligible to play football for a period of one year. The plaintiff brought action to set aside the ruling of the association, but he was unsuccessful. *Morrison v. Roberts,* 82 P.2d 1023 (Okla. 1938). The court held that the boy had many rights as a citizen and as a high school student, but he had no vested right to "eligibility" in the state's high school athletic association. These cases are in harmony with the thinking of the majority of the courts with respect to voluntary associations.

72 *Control of Personnel by the School Board*

Plaintiff-teacher was a physical education instructor for more than 35 years, and was on tenure. He applied for a leave of absence and submitted a physician's certificate to the effect that he had been advised to refrain from work for six to nine months because of his medical status. He requested time to re-establish his physical stamina. He was district manager of an encyclopedia firm, and had been selling books during the summer months. He had been informed by the company that if he were to remain in that capacity he would have to work full time. The board granted the leave but attached the condition that plaintiff was not to engage in any gainful employment during the time of the leave. Nevertheless, the plaintiff took leave and while on leave continued to work for the publishing firm as a sales manager. When he returned, plaintiff was requested to sign an affidavit to the effect he had engaged in no gainful employment; this he refused to do, so the board rescinded the new contract and offered plaintiff re-employment at a beginning teacher's salary.

Relief Sought: To test the validity of a contract of employment

Issue: Can the board legally restrict a tenured teacher's leave of absence?

Holding of the Trial Court: Dismissed plaintiff's case

Holding of the Appellate Court: Affirmed

Reasoning

The condition of the leave of absence was not oppressive or harsh. Plaintiff knew that he was not supposed to work at gainful employment. He also had agreed to accept the leave on the conditions laid down by the board. Tenure is for the benefit both of the school system and of the teachers. The board may reasonably place restrictions on leaves of absence which will protect the interests of both parties. The plaintiff was free to work or to cast about for a more desirable job if he chose but at the risk of losing his tenure. It is not oppressive or harsh when one must face the fact that "one cannot have his cake and eat it too."

Significance

The school board may reasonably restrict the teacher's use of leaves of absence by placing conditions upon its exercise designed to promote the interests of the school.

CASE CITATION: *Liddicoat v. Kenosha City Board of Education, 117 N.W.2d 369 (Wisc. 1962)*

AUTHOR'S COMMENTARY

Providing leaves of absence to school personnel for professional improvement or health reasons is a legitimate exercise of the board's power to employ personnel and improve them on the job. Even in the absence of a state statute permitting or mandating such practice, it is generally held that the board has this power.

The question of what may constitute a reasonable restraint upon the use of this leave of absence has not generated much litigation. In Indiana, a teacher on tenure declared his candidacy for state office. The board immediately passed a resolution that any school employee elected to public office would be required to take a leave of absence without pay. The teacher brought an action to recover the salary lost through enforcement of the resolution, but he was unsuccessful. Said the court:

> This rule, general in terms and applying to all teachers, does not to us seem such an unreasonable exercise of the board's powers as to warrant judicial interference. The board, not the courts, is charged with the duty of managing the school system, and so long as it acts with fairness its decisions on matters within its discretion are not subject to

judicial review. *School City of East Chicago v. Sigler,* 36 N.E.2d 760 (Ind. 1941)

73   *The Reach of the Common Law*

The United States Supreme Court on June 17, 1963 handed down a pair of decisions declaring unconstitutional the Pennsylvania statute and the Baltimore board's resolution to require the reading of the Bible and the offering of prayers daily in the public schools. Nevertheless, despite an attorney general's opinion to the contrary, a local board passed a resolution to the effect that Bible reading was not to be discontinued. The apparent ground for the resolution was that the decisions of the U. S. Supreme Court were not directly applicable to the New Jersey statutes. As a result of this resolution, there was widespread indecision in the state as to the applicability of the Court's decisions to New Jersey statutes and practices. Relief was sought by the attorney general on the grounds that principals, teachers, and parents did not know what to do. Teachers had taken an oath to support the U. S. Constitution so were doubtful of their duty as employees of the board of education.

Relief Sought: Injunction to prevent local board from carrying out a resolution to the effect that Bible reading was not to be halted

Issue: Does one have to be party to a decision to be bound thereby?

Holding of the Trial Court: For the board

Holding of the Appellate Court: Reversed

Reasoning

On their face, the *Abington* and *Murray* decisions would appear to apply to the New Jersey statutes. That one does not have to be a party to a decision to be bound thereby is a doctrine of long standing. The directive by the attorney general and the Commissioner of Education has been directly flaunted by defendants (the board). The impression which this made or will make on the children of Hawthorne cannot be measured with precision. Those who incite and encourage disrespect for the law are as equally responsible as those who actually commit the violation. Public officials must set the standard for behavior. They cannot war against the Constitution. If they hold the legal process in contempt, this defiance can result only in barbarism. This is their responsibility in every city of the United States. They must assist the courts to infuse faith in the "Supreme Law of the Land." If the majority believe that prayer and Bible reading should become part of our way of life in public schools, then they must do whatever is legally necessary to regain this privilege.

Significance

One does not have to be a party to a decision handed down by the courts to be bound thereby. School officials, of all people, should be careful to respect the law and uphold it at all times, not only because this is expected of public officials, but also because they deal with citizens of young and impressionable age. Public officials must set the standard for behavior.

CASE CITATION: *Sills v. Board of Education of Hawthorne, 200 A.2d 817 (N.J. 1963)*

AUTHOR'S COMMENTARY

A similar case which arose in Massachusetts about the same time is to the same effect. *Attorney General v. School Committee of North Brookfield,* 199 N.E.2d 553 (Mass. 1964).

Clearly the board had in mind no desire to deliberately break the law, but by its resolution it placed the teachers in an untenable position. Were they to obey the board resolution and continue Bible reading, or disregard the oath they had taken to uphold the Constitution at all times? Teachers might be liable to federal criminal prosecution for compliance with the resolution. Furthermore, teaching in open defiance of the fact that the Supreme Court had overthrown religious practices in public schools in adjoining states is not only illegal, but amounts to indefensible moral instruction for the youth of the state.

The Supreme Court of New Jersey noted that the facts and relevant laws in *Abington* and *Murray* (see Case No. 16 *supra*) were almost identical to the New Jersey statutes in question. It did not matter that the New Jersey statutes specifically in question had never been declared unconstitutional.

74 Right to Dismiss Teachers

Arizona law does not list specific causes for tenure teacher dismissal, but teachers in that state may be dismissed upon a determination that "there existed good and just cause for the notice of dismissal." Good and just cause may not include religious and political beliefs or affiliations "unless in violation of the oath of the teacher." Plaintiff was a tenured teacher dismissed by the board on the ground that she had become a center of controversy in the school district, and that parents threatened to withdraw their children from school if she remained as teacher. Plaintiff sought reinstatement to her position and back pay for the time she was idle.

Relief Sought: Reinstatement to the position of teacher

Issue: May a teacher be dismissed for becoming "a center of controversy"?

Holding of the Trial Court: For the board

Holding of the Appellate Court: Reversed

Reasoning

The Supreme Court of the State of Arizona commented that the evidence showed that the teacher had indeed become "the focus of a community squabble." The community was divided on several incidents none, of which was sufficient in themselves to justify the discharge of a continuing teacher. The central question under the Teacher Tenure Act is whether being the center of controversy constitutes a good cause for the teacher's dismissal. Quoting from *Paul v. Sch. Dist.,* 28 Vt. 575 (1856) in which a teacher was accused of being cross, crusty and severe, "there is no connection between complaints by parents and incompetency in teachers. A mere accident will set the community off. . . . But if the teacher chooses to persist . . . we do not perceive how he can be deprived of his contract to go on with the school without a claim to damages for the loss he thereby sustains. . . ." It is not reasonable to require the rigors of school teaching, for less wages, it may be, and often is, than he would command in the most ordinary agricultural or mechanical employments. Quoting from *Anthony v. Phoenix Union High School,* 100 P.2d 988 (Ariz. 1940): "Teachers who break the law may be removed, not because of the complaints of parents, but because his actions impair the efficiency of the school." This was not true in the instant case. There is always a certain amount of rumor and hearsay but these are inadmissible in a court of law. The parents might have gone and seen for themselves, and, if they did not, they should not now request this court to condemn the plaintiff upon the imperfect and unsatisfactory ground upon which they are content to rely. They might act upon hearsay, but courts have to require proof.

Significance

Teachers may not be dismissed because of the fact they become centers of controversy in the community.

CASE CITATION: *Kersey v. Maine Consolidated School District No. 10, 394 P.2d 201 (Ariz. 1964)*

AUTHOR'S COMMENTARY

Courts will ordinarily not interfere in controversy between the board and one of its employees, unless there is evidence that a civil or contractual right is being violated. A teacher who is gruff, crusty and given to strong language is not necessarily incompetent, said the court in *Paul*:

> And among men of medium ability, and that is all which a contract of this kind requires for its performance, among such teachers, as a general thing, perhaps, very often, certainly, the most artful and intriguing, or indulgent, and who care little about the result of their service, if they only get through and get pay, are about as likely, perhaps, to give a sort of negative satisfaction to the pupils, and to the parents, often, as those who sincerely and studiously labor to control the school, and to teach the pupils thoroughly, and govern them with reasonable strictness. So that knowing of complaints in school is no certain proof of fault in the teacher; we must still inquire further. We are in fact no nearer the ultimate truth of the matter. . . . If there is great dissatisfaction, there is more commonly some fault upon both sides. *Paul v. Sch. Dist. No. 2,* 28 Vt. 575 (1856) at p. 581.

Teacher dismissal cases are the most numerous of all school law litigation. Much of this litigation need not have been tested in the courts but for no better manner in which to settle educational conflict. Perhaps with the advent of collective bargaining in the schools, much of this costly and time-consuming litigation may be shifted over to the grievance machinery ordinarily found in the school district having a written agreement with its teachers' organizations.

75 *Compliance with Controlling Statutory Law*

Plaintiff was a resident taxpayer who challenged the election at which bonds were authorized. The statute provides that certain steps be taken to publicize the election such as that at least five days prior to the date the board shall publish in a newspaper and post in five conspicuous places in the district a notice of election following a prescribed form. The board did not publish an official notice, but a news story was published and the school officials posted five conspicuous places in the district. In addition, the superintendent mailed out a brochure to each boxholder in the district. The brochure contained general information about the need for the bonds, who was eligible to vote, and other pertinent data. The election was held as scheduled and carried. However, a taxpayer sought to challenge the election, but was nonsuited by the trial court. Plaintiff appealed and the case was finally before the Supreme Court of New Mexico which held for the taxpaying plaintiff.

Relief Sought: Injunction to prevent the school board from issuing and selling school bonds

Issue: Was a school bond election invalid where substantial rather than complete compliance with the controlling statute was involved?

Holding of the Trial Court: Complaint dismissed

Holding of the Appellate Court: Reversed

Reasoning

The question is not one of substantial compliance. It is claimed that the giving of general notice is sufficient. We are unable, however, to agree with this contention. The statute plainly provides that notice of the school election "shall" be published as therein provided. The phrase used is mandatory. Newspaper articles and comments or publicity by television or radio cannot lawfully substitute for the mandatory requirements. It is commendable that the board made an attempt to acquaint the voters with all of the aspects of the proposed bond issue, but the legislature has stated that notice shall be made by posting and by publication in a newspaper and we hold that this statute is controlling in this case. Although the board complied with the posting requirement, the failure to publish as required by the statutes vitiates the election.

Significance

School boards must comply fully with the exact letter of the law governing school bond elections if their efforts are to succeed. Substantial compliance is not enough; it must go all the way. By failing to publish notice in a newspaper as required by statute, the board "had it all to do over again." The second time, it might not be as successful in gaining the required votes for passage.

CASE CITATION: *Wiggins v. Lopez, 387 P.2d 330 (N.Mex. 1963)*

76 Compulsory Attendance

Defendant was father of a 15 year old girl and a member of the Amish faith. He was sentenced to pay a fine of $5.00 and costs for failure to send his daughter to school as required by law in Kansas. The daughter had completed the eighth grade and was enrolled as a high school student in a correspondence course school in Chicago. She was making good grades. State law required school attendance till age 16. Amish farmers had established the Harmony school for those who had completed the eighth grade. Formal classes were held one morning per week, and students spent the remainder of the week at home in study and vocational training, according to their faith. Defendant was a member of the Old Order Amish Mennonite Church, and believed that secular influences should be avoided in the education of their youth. A cardinal tenet of the Amish faith is the Biblical injunction, "Be not conformed to this world." The order was opposed to public secondary education because it would corrupt their children and erode the Amish way of life.

> *Relief Sought:* Exemption from the compulsory attendance laws and substitution of another means of educating youth

> *Issue:* Was defendant parent guilty of any offense and did the compulsory attendance laws violate defendant's constitutionally guaranteed religious freedom?

> *Holding of the Trial Court:* Found guilty and fine imposed

> *Holding of the Kansas Supreme Court:* Affirmed

Reasoning

The child is not the mere creature of the state; his parents have the right to decide by what means he shall be educated. *Pierce v. Society of Sisters,* 268 U.S. 510 (Ore. 1925). Exemptions from the compulsory attendance law are made only on the basis of physical or mental incapacity, an exemption not pleaded by defendant. His defense was that his daughter's schooling was equal to that in the public schools. We have had compulsory attendance laws in Kansas since 1874. Defendant, no matter how sincere or well intentioned, must be deemed guilty of violating the statute. The statute does not invade the defendant's religious freedom. There was no contention that the law was unconstitutional, hence it is to be assumed that it is so. Parents have the right to educate their children elsewhere than in the public schools only when the means utilized meet the state's minimum educational requirements. "Religious liberty includes the absolute right to believe but only a limited right to act." *Commonwealth v. Beiler,* 79 A.2d 134 (Pa. 1956).

Significance

The parent may educate his child outside the public schools, but the method he chooses must be equal to that which the child would receive in the public schools. The burden of proof is with the parent. Such a compulsory attendance law does not invade the religious liberty which the parent has to believe, which is absolute, nor his right to act, which is limited.

CASE CITATION: *State v. Garber, 419 P.2d 896 (Kans. 1966)*

AUTHOR'S COMMENTARY

On the issue of religious freedom the court said:

In accommodating between the competing right of the state to compel action in the public welfare and the right of the individual to his constitutional religious freedom the courts have distinguished between religious beliefs and religious practices. Failure to comply with reasonable requirements in the exercise of the police power for the general welfare has never been condoned in the name of religious freedom.

The leading case on this topic is *Commonwealth v. Beiler,* 79 A.2d 134, (Pa. 1956) in which the court had this to say about religious exercise:

Religious liberty includes absolute right to believe but only a limited right to act. . . . Thus, a Mormon believed that plural marriages were divinely inspired, but when he acted upon his belief, he was convicted of polygamy. A Jew held his Sabbath a holy day, but when he refused to be judicially sworn on Saturday, he was fined. A Seventh Day Baptist believed he should rest from his labors on Saturday and follow the divine command, "six days shalt thou labor," but when he worked on Sunday, he was convicted under the blue laws. A Mennonite maid believed she should wear the distinctive garb of her Church at all times, but she was not allowed to wear it in her school. An imposing list of similar cases might be compiled.

The parent thus has the right to worship the Supreme Being according to the dictates of his own heart; to adopt any creed or hold any opinion whatever on the subject of religion; and to do, or to forebear to do, any act, for conscience sake, the doing of which or the forebearance of which is not prejudicial to the public weal. But *salus populi suprema lex* (the safety of the commonwealth is the highest law) is a maxim of universal application; and where liberty of conscience would impinge on the paramount right of the public, it ought to be restrained.

No matter how sincere he may be, the individual cannot be permitted on religious grounds to be the judge of his duty to obey the laws which were enacted in the public interest. Thus, compulsory attendance laws do not invade the religious liberty of the individual parent who does not believe in secular education.

After struggling with the Amish problem for some years, the Iowa Legislature in 1967 enacted a statute excluding members of this sect from the state's compulsory attendance law, with the stipulation, however, that the state superintendent of public instruction may give exempted children certain tests on an annual basis to determine how well the plan is working. These cases and the action taken by the Iowa Legislature illustrate Americans' belief in *salus populi suprema lex* and in the ascendancy of the use of the public school attendance laws to achieve basic American liberties.

77 *Board's Power to Make Up Its Own Mind*

Pershing School District No. 6 had a three-member board of education operating one elementary school. The schoolhouse was destroyed by fire, creating a problem of what to do with the children for the ensuing year. Plaintiffs were parents of the children who sought to compel the board to acquire and provide a used school building to replace the one destroyed. South Dakota law provides that at a special meeting, electors of the district may give binding instructions to the school board, provided that the subject of such instructions shall have been advertised in the notice of the meeting. Under this part of the law, a meeting was held on July 28, and the board was instructed, after receiving legal notice, to purchase a used school building and install it in the district. The instructions given to the board at the meeting did not specify the used school to be purchased, nor did it designate or limit the amount the board was to spend or the school year for which the building was to be furnished.

Relief Sought: Mandamus to compel the board to provide a school building to replace one destroyed by fire

> *Issue:* May the courts interfere in the decision-making area of board operation where the thing in question is discretionary in nature?
>
> *Holding of the Trial Court:* Writ granted
>
> *Holding of the South Dakota Supreme Court:* Suit dismissed

Reasoning

Even assuming that the board had been directed to provide the used building for the school year 1964–65, the duty imposed on the school board by the instructions given at the special meeting were not ministerial in character. Because of the indefiniteness of the electors' instructions, the board, in carrying out the mandate given it, was required to exercise discretion. Of necessity it had to use its own judgment in deciding what schoolhouse it would purchase since none was specified in the instructions. Surely it could not be expected to acquire one that was not suitable for the needs of the district or one that the members of the board honestly felt required the expenditure of an exorbitant amount of the district's funds. Mandamus is usually available to force the board to perform ministerial duties. But when utilized in such instances, "the court is not warranted in directing the manner in which a legal discretion shall be exercised."

Significance

Courts will not interfere to direct the board in the manner in which discretionary powers vested in the school board are to be exercised. Where the legislature has given the choice to the board, courts will not intercede unless there was evidence of fraud, collusion, or illegal procedures on the part of the board.

CASE CITATION: *Dejong v. School Board of Common School District, 135 N.W.2d 726 (S.Dak. 1965)*

78 Board Practice of Requiring Photograph of Teaching Applicants

The Board Against Discrimination of the State of Washington enacted a regulation (WAC 162-16-010) pertaining to the practice of requiring a pre-employment photograph of applicants for jobs in the public schools. Despite this regulation, certain school districts continued to require such photograph and a test case was arranged. A hearing tribunal appointed by the Board Against Discrimination found that the Olympia school district was in violation of the regulation. "The attaching of the photograph is a graphic specification of the applicant's race or color, as much or more than the affixing of the words 'Negro' or 'Oriental' would be."

Relief Sought: Injunction against the practice of requiring a photograph of all applicants for a teaching job in the district

Issue: May the legislature delegate to an administrative body of its own creation discretionary power over other subdivisions of state government such as school districts?

Holding of the Trial Court: For the Board Against Discrimination

Holding of the Appellate Court: Affirmed

Reasoning

The school board contends that a "simple request for a photograph" does not express an intent to violate state laws against discrimination. A personal interview, said the board, would reveal the applicant's race more effectively and more certainly than the photograph, hence the evil sought to be remedied would not be remedied. We see no merit in any of the school board's contentions. It seems clear that the legislature intended to withhold from the school board the right to hire only certain races, and we hold that the court below had no jurisdiction to entertain this question. The resolution of the Board Against Discrimination is controlling.

Significance

If the legislature chooses to create an administrative body, such as the Board Against Discrimination, and delegate some of its powers to such a body, the school board cannot legitimately complain, since the legislature has plenary (complete) power over education in the state.

CASE CITATION: *Washington State Board Against Discrimination v. Olympia School District, 412 P.2d 769 (Wash. 1966)*

79   Defamation of Character

The president of the board of education wrote an allegedly libelous letter to a school patron, who then brought an action naming the board president, the editor of one newspaper in which the letter appeared, and the receiver of another newspaper. In her defense, the board president asserted that she wrote and published the letter "for the purpose of defending her own reputation against numerous charges and allegations published by the plaintiff." Soon thereafter, the board met and adopted a resolution that at the time of the writing of the letter, she was acting on behalf of the board of education, and was in fact acting as its chief executive officer. The resolution directed the board's legal counsel "to vigorously (sic) defend said suit" and transferred $1,500 to the legal account, presumably to pay the fee. Thereupon, plaintiff brought this suit. The question was whether the president's action in writing the letter could be considered as in the performance of a duty of the board of education. Motion to dismiss was denied and defendants appealed.

Relief Sought: Injunction to prevent expenditure of public school moneys to defend the school board president in a libel suit

Issue: May a local school board expend school funds for the legal defense of one of its members?

Holding of the Trial Court: Refused to dismiss

Holding of the Appellate Court: For plaintiff

Reasoning

The letter writing was not in the line of duty. When a public official is sued individually for libel, it must be shown that he was performing in good faith a duty of his office or position in furtherance of the work of the board for which he was purportedly acting. The defendant's personal reply to plaintiff's letters in defense of her own reputation cannot reasonably be regarded as the performance of a public duty imposed or authorized by law, even though the subject matter which induced the letter writing related to a proposed site for a new school. When a school officer or member of a board of education does a wrongful or negligent act, whereby injury to another results, he is liable therefore, not because he is a school official or board member, but because he is the person doing the act.

Significance

School board members should avoid publication of information about third parties unless it is clear that it is in the line of duty. By failing to observe this simple rule, they may step outside the protection of their office and become personally liable where statements have been made which result in defaming another.

CASE CITATION: *Errington v. Mansfield Township Board of Education, 195 A.2d 670 (N.J. 1963)*

80 School Records

The school board adopted a resolution that parents would be permitted to inspect the records of their children, including progress reports, subject grades, intelligence quotients, test scores, achievement scores, and medical, psychological and psychiatric reports. The State Commissioner of Education held that the parent could inspect the contents of the record with appropriate school personnel present to interpret the records to the parents. The courts did not fully agree with the Commissioner's ruling, but held nevertheless that parents might inspect school records "of their children as persons in interest."

Relief Sought: Mandamus to require school officials to reveal the contents of son's school records

Issue: Are school pupil personnel records "public"?

Holding of the Trial Court: For plaintiff

Holding of the Appellate Court: Affirmed

Reasoning

The records here sought to be inspected are not, strictly speaking, public records. No statute exists which specifies those who are and those who are not entitled to inspect them. The records are required by law to be kept. It needs no further citation of authority to recognize the obvious "interest" which a parent has in the school records of his child. We are, therefore, constrained to hold as a matter of law that the parent is entitled to inspect the records.

Significance

Although a student record is not a public record in the legal meaning of that term, it is at least a "quasi-public" record, and parents, as persons of interest, may have access to the contents of their child's record during office hours.

CASE CITATION: *Van Allen v. McCleary, 211 N.Y.S.2d 501 (N.Y. 1961)*

AUTHOR'S COMMENTARY

The law is constantly concerned with the balance between the public's right to know and the individual's right to privacy. Neither completely "open records" nor completely closed records would be acceptable; rather, a compromise is necessary between these two extremes if the interests of society and individuals are to be protected. The courts must decide where this fine line of distinction should be drawn, as for example, in a case which arose in Iowa. *Valentine v. Independent School District,* 174 N.W. 334 (Iowa 1919). A high school senior had completed her work for graduation, but refused to wear a cap and gown to commencement exercises. She was denied her diploma and grades. The superintendent of schools maintained that the grades were his property, and no one had access to them. In a suit to obtain the grades, the girl was successful. The court said that the grades were not the property of the school, but were "public records" within the meaning of the law.

In *People v. Peller,* 181 N.E.2d 376 (Ill. 1962) some taxpayers sought to examine school board records for the years 1955 through 1960, and obtained the records from the board. The board, however, balked at having photographs made of the records. The court held that "good public policy requires liberality in the right to examine public records," and permitted the use of the camera in recording the data.

Many states now have "open records laws" which require the disclosure of public records, including student and teacher personnel files, to "persons in interest." Any attempt to generalize on the status of pupil records as "public" records would therefore not only be fruitless but dangerous, since each jurisdiction is a province unto itself. School officials should acquaint themselves with the attitude of the legislature and courts toward student records in each respective state.

81 *Extra-Class Assignments for Teachers*

Plaintiff was a teacher who was assigned to sponsor, in addition to his regular classroom duties, a boys' bowling club for the school year. The bowling sessions—which took place at a privately operated bowling establishment located approximately one and one-half miles from the high school where he taught—occurred after school hours one day per week during the school term, each session lasting about two and one-half hours. The public school did not bear the costs, each boy paying his own transportation to the establishment as well as the cost of his individual bowling. There were no intra-mural nor interscholastic bowling teams with which to compete and the club did not get credit for participating. It was not intended that the teacher instruct in bowling but simply that he sponsor the group and be in attendance while the bowling took place. The teacher refused the assignment and was dismissed, whereupon he sought clarification of his status in court.

Relief Sought: Reinstatement to the position of teacher and clarification of his work status

Issue: Must a teacher accept an extra-class assignment which has no direct relationship to the school program?

Holding of the Trial Court: For defendant board

Holding of the Appellate Court: Reversed

Reasoning

School teachers must realize that they are subject to assignment by the school board to any activity directly related to the school program; classroom duties in school hours do not constitute all their duties. On the other hand, school boards must realize that their power of assignment of school teachers to extracurricular duties is not without limitation and restriction; under (the applicable statute) the activity to which a school teacher is assigned must be related to the school program, and the assignment must be fairly and reasonably made. Because the extra-class assignment here involved had no relationship to the school's program of studies, the board may not make the assignment in question, and therefore plaintiff's refusal to accept it could not be considered as incompetency so as to justify his removal.

Significance

Boards have the right to assign teachers to extra-curricular activities where the work to be done has some reasonable relationship to the ongoing school program, but where this is not present, the teacher may legally refuse the assignment in question.

CASE CITATION: *Pease v. Millcreek Township School District, 195 A.2d. 104 (Pa. 1963)*

AUTHOR'S COMMENTARY

In another Pennsylvania case, the refusal of a temporary teacher (one not on tenure) to attend a school's "Open House" constituted insubordination and was sufficient grounds on which the board was justified in removing her following a hearing. *Johnson v. United School District,* 191 A.2d 897 (Pa. 1963). A teacher who refused to lead his students in a civil defense shelter drill was legally dismissed. *National Education Association Journal,* December, 1963, p. 5. Similarly, a school board rule requiring male teachers to attend certain football and basketball games and supervise students in the stands was held to be a reasonable exercise of the board's power. *McGrath v. Burkhard,* 280 P.2d 864 (Calif. 1955). These cases seem to be in agreement that the board may within reason require more than just classroom performance of the public school teacher as a part of his contractual obligation of employment.

Teachers' contracts ordinarily do not include such assignments on their face but it is well settled in the law that all board rules and regulations are included in the contract under the doctrine of incorporation by reference. Thus, one cannot determine what constitutes a day's work in teaching merely by reading the contract of employment.

The statement by the court in the "open house" case above is indicative of the way the courts feel about the teacher's obligations under the contract:

The open house is a significant part of the school program. Good teachers, sometimes accepting the annoyance of a few unreasonable parents, appreciate the opportunity which the open house gives them to explain the school program to the parents and to learn more about the pupils. Refusal, without cause, of a new teacher to participate in this program sets a bad example for the students, is an annoyance to the faithful teachers who always participate, is embarrassing to the school officials who are called upon to explain her absence, and disappointing if not outright disgusting to the parents and relatives who have made personal sacrifices to be there. Any school teacher who lacks an understanding of her responsibility to be present on this occasion, and who arrogantly refuses to obey the direction of her employer to be there and instead follows her own personal whims and pleasures can properly be held by the board employing her to be unfit to continue in the employment of the board. *Johnson v. United School District,* 191 A.2d 897 (Pa. 1963).

82   *Appearance of Teachers*

Plaintiff was a male teacher who had grown a beard and wanted to wear it in a high school where there was a rule against beards and moustaches worn by students. When he refused after a conference with the principal to remove the beard, he was transferred to home teaching. The principal claimed that to allow plaintiff to wear the beard in school would encourage students to imitate his example and thus violate the rule. The principal further said he thought the teacher was wearing the beard to create an incident. The Court of Appeals, Second District, held the transfer was illegal. "A beard, for a man, is an expression of his personality," said the court, "and is protected under the First and Fourteenth Amendments."

Relief Sought: Reinstatement to the position of classroom teacher

Issue: May a male teacher wear a beard while performing his usual duties in the classroom?

Holding of the Trial Court: For plaintiff

Holding of the Appellate Court: Affirmed

Reasoning

As a matter of actual experience, there is nothing in the record to show that the wearing of beards by male teachers did disrupt or impair classroom discipline or the teaching process. The benefit to be realized by the restriction does not outweigh the resulting impairment of plaintiff's constitutional right to wear such a beard. A beard cannot be changed after school hours as can wearing apparel. This is not to say that all male teachers at all high schools, regardless of circumstances, may wear beards while they teach in classrooms and that the practice may not be prohibited or otherwise restrained under appropriate circumstances. What we do hold is simply that, on the record before us, with the complete absence of any actual experience at the high school involved as to what the actual adverse effect of the wearing of a beard by a male teacher would be upon the conduct of the educational processes there, beards as such, on male teachers, without regard to their general appearance, their neatness and their cleanliness, cannot constitutionally be banned from the classroom and from the campus.

Significance

The board may not "yell before it is hurt." If, however, after a fair trial test, if it proves disruptive, a beard may be challenged on the grounds that it impairs the educational process or creates a disruption of discipline in the school.

CASE CITATION: *Finot v. Pasadena City Board of Education, 58 Cal.Rptr. 520 (Calif. 1967)*

AUTHOR'S COMMENTARY

In *Blanchet v. Vermilion Parish School Board,* 220 So.2d 534 (La. 1969), the Louisiana Court of Appeals upheld a school board regulation requiring male teachers to wear neckties. The court said that the board's regulation was reasonable inasmuch as the wearing of neckties is the conventional attire of business and professional men. The court also stated that a tenured teacher may be disciplined or discharged for failure to comply with a reasonable regulation properly adopted by the board of education.

It is not clear whether teachers may be required to wear skirts longer than the mini-variety, but any board regulation concerning dress and appearance of teachers must be reasonable. What is reasonable in any given circumstance is for the jury.

In New York, the Acting Commissioner of Education ruled that school officials may not take disciplinary action against male teachers simply because they disapprove of their hair or moustaches. Similarly, in Massachusetts a United States District Court has ordered a school board to re-employ and pay back salary to a male teacher dismissed for wearing a beard, *Lucia v. Duggan,* 303 F.Supp. 112, 1969.

83   *Circulating Petitions During School Hours*

On January 30, 1967, the Los Angeles Teachers Union distributed to its representatives in the 600 elementary and secondary schools in the Los Angeles Public School District a petition directed to certain California state officials protesting a threatened cutback in state funds for higher education in California. The next day, the central office notified the administrators in its district that circulation of the petition was contrary to a board rule and instructed them to prohibit its circulation. The union thereupon brought suit to challenge the board's rule. The trial court held for the school board and the union appealed. The California appellate court affirmed, and the teachers' union again appealed. This time, the California Supreme Court reversed and said that "teachers, like others, have the right to speak freely and effectively on public questions as well as the 'inseparable' and 'cognate' right to petition the Government for a redress of grievances. They do not shed these rights at the schoolhouse gate."

Relief Sought: Mandamus to force the board to permit the circulation of a petition among teachers during school hours

Issue: May the board of education deny teachers the right to circulate a petition of general interest during school hours?

Holding of the Trial Court: For defendants

Holding of the California Supreme Court: Reversed

Reasoning

While school authorities have broad authority to prescribe and control conduct in the schools, the courts must strike a balance between the interests of the teacher, as a citizen, in commenting upon matters of public concern and the interest of the State, as an employer, in promoting the efficiency of the public services it performs through its employees. A school board is under a constitutional requirement to be tolerant of the unrest intrinsic to the expression of controversial ideas. If a school board acts to restrict free speech rights of teachers, the school officials must produce facts which might reasonably have led them to forecast *substantial disruption of or material interference with school activities.* (Emphasis supplied by the Court.) The Los Angeles School Board did not produce such facts, nor did it prove that circulation of the teachers' petition posed a significant threat to efficiency and integrity of the public service.

Significance

If the board would limit the circulation of a petition during school hours, its burden of proof that such an exercise of a fundamental liberty by its employees may be such a burden that the board would find it quite difficult if not indeed impossible to carry. "Controversy . . . must be tolerated in the schools as well as in society generally."

CASE CITATION: *Los Angeles Teachers Union v. Los Angeles City Board of Education, 455 P.2d 827 (Calif. 1969)*

84   School Board Powers

Plaintiff student attended a high school where there was a yearly charge of $25.00 on each of the pupils, one-half of which was called "textbook fees" and the other half was described as "school activity fees." Plaintiff refused to pay the fees but was permitted to attend high school and graduate. He was provided textbooks, and furnished a cap and gown and a diploma upon graduation, notwithstanding his failure to pay the $25.00. When he applied for admission to Idaho State University, his former high school refused to send his transcripts because of the non-payment. He brought an action to compel the high school to send his grade transcript to the university. The trial court ordered issuance, and the school district appealed.

> *Relief Sought:* Action to compel high school to issue plaintiff's grades

Issue: Is a fee invalid where the state constitution provides that schools shall be free?

Holding of the Trial Court: For plaintiff

Holding of the Idaho Supreme Court: Affirmed

Reasoning

The Idaho State Constitution calls for "a general, uniform and thorough system of public, free common schools." We hold that a high school comes within this definition, and therefore the fee is invalid. It should be noted that, because social and extra-curricular activities are not necessary elements of a high school career, the constitution does not prohibit the board from setting fees to cover costs of such activities to be paid by students who wish to exercise an option to participate in them. However, a school might charge a fee for the transfer of credits which bears a "relationship to the actual costs of printing and distributing the transcripts."

Significance

Although the constitution specifies that the state's schools shall be "free," a reasonable fee may be charged for instances in which the students opt to participate in extra-curricular, non-required activities, and such a fee does not violate the constitution.

CASE CITATION: *Paulson v. Minidoka County School District, 463 P.2d 935 (Ida. 1970)*

PART SIX

Racial Discrimination,
Religious Freedom,
and Dismissal Cases

Part Six

Racial Discrimination, Religious Freedom, and Dismissal Cases

The seventeen cases contained in this section round out the book and fill the "holidays" not otherwise covered in the five earlier sections of the present volume. Two of the cases pertain to the work of the guidance counselor, while another relates to the concept of "due process" in dismissal proceedings. The cases are grouped to heighten their effect, and to help the reader compare and/or contrast decisions in related areas.

Three of the cases in this section deal with questions of church-state relationships. Although other states have chosen to provide public funds for private and sectarian institutions, the Supreme Court of Hawaii (see Case No. 85) with the insights obtained from a comparatively recent Constitutional Convention, chose instead to reject the "child benefit" theory, and insist that the term "all school children" should apply to all *public* school children only in determining beneficiaries of the state's bus transportation provision. Another decision tests the legality of a nativity scene on school property, while the third pertains to the legality of baccalaureate services in the public schools.

When the United States Supreme Court handed down the *Brown* decision in 1954, it realized that a century of segregation in the public schools would not be easy to overcome; hence, in its second *Brown* decision, it placed the handling of these cases arising under *Brown* securely in the hands of the federal courts. This "enforcement decree" is less well known than the first decision, but quite important for the schoolman to understand. It is listed here as Case No. 86.

Teachers' rights in contrast with board powers are explored in five of the cases in this section, especially as related to the right of the board to dismiss the teacher from employment in the district. One case deals with the growing problem of homosexuality, handled here in a case arising in California. You may not agree with the board's holding that homosexual behavior cannot be grounds for teacher dismissal unless there is evidence that it interferes with the ability of the teacher to teach. The point to be emphasized here is that the board must "do its homework" well, or it will find to its dismay that it has failed in its efforts to rid the staff of questionable individuals.

The "burden of proof" in such court proceedings, being upon the board of education, has placed a very heavy evidentiary burden upon the board, which is in some cases fatal to the board's case in court. To be emphasized is the necessity for the board to go into court well prepared, and replete with legal counsel of the highest quality. No other approach will yield the dividends and regain the lost prestige, if not indeed the actual power, which school boards are rapidly losing in such legal entanglements. While this suggests continuing legal counsel, such an approach might be expensive to support, and difficult to justify to the constituency. Retaining on an annual basis competent legal counsel, with authorization to engage outside help in cases of litigation, seems a sound course to follow in these explosive times.

85 *Transporting Parochial Pupils at Public Expense*

In 1965, under a new constitution, the state took over many functions previously performed by the county units, among them transportation of school children. Under Act 233, effective June 6, 1967, the Legislature authorized the State Department of Education to "provide suitable transportation for all school children in grades Kg. to 12 and in special education classes." During fiscal 1967, the sum of $54,610.70 was disbursed by the State Comptroller for transportation of both public and non-public school children. Plaintiffs brought this action seeking a determination of the legality of this payment to other than public schools. The trial court rendered judgment for the defendants and plaintiffs appealed. The Supreme Court of Hawaii held that the payments to private schools were invalid.

Relief Sought: Declaratory judgment and injunctive relief challenging use of public funds to provide bus transportation subsidies to sectarian and private school students

Issue: Does the legislative authorization to transport "all school children" apply to nonpublic as well as to public school children?

Holding of the Trial Court: For defendant

Holding of the Hawaii Supreme Court: Reversed

Reasoning

Article IX, Section 1 of the Constitution of the State of Hawaii provides that no public funds shall be "appropriated for the support or benefit of any sectarian or private educational institution." Defendants maintain that the benefit is to the child, and not the sectarian institution (the "child-benefit theory"), and cite cases to support same. (See Cases Nos. 9, 10 and 17 *supra*). The burden of proof that a rule or statute is unconstitutional is on the one who brings the suit to challenge, here the plaintiffs-appellants. We find that appellants have met this requirement. Our Constitutional Convention of 1950 specifically rejected the child benefit theory as applied to bus transportation and similar general welfare programs for nonpublic school students. Our state private school system is stronger than anywhere else in the United States, whereas public schools have received somewhat shabby treatment by the Legislature. The language of the Constitution is unequivocal: "Nor shall public funds be appropriated for the support or benefit of any sectarian or private educational institution." This it means, despite the use of such funds for dental and public health services to private school pupils. The Constitution ties the hands of the Legislature, and prohibits it from making any appropriation aiding a sectarian or private school, including subsidies for bus transportation. The term "all school children" referred to in the act means "all public school children," but not to nonpublic school children. The Legislature must return to the people to ask them to decide whether their State Constitution should be amended to grant the Legislature the power that it seeks. This course of action was followed in New York and New Jersey, and must be followed here if the power to provide "support and benefit" to nonpublic schools is given the Legislative body.

Significance

Narrowly interpreting its new state constitution, the Supreme Court of Hawaii has ruled that the state may not provide bus transportation to both nonpublic and private schools, but must confine its support to public schools only.

CASE CITATION: *Spears v. Honda, 449 P.2d 130 (Hawaii 1968)*

86 Desegregation of the Public Schools

The four cases which arose in connection with *Brown* were from a variety of local conditions; therefore, the Supreme Court sought the help of the

Attorneys General of the United States and the states requiring or permitting racial discrimination in public education to present their views on the question. The parties, the United States, and the States of Florida, North Carolina, Arkansas, Oklahoma, Maryland, and Texas filed briefs and participated in the oral argument. In carrying out the intent of *Brown,* school authorities have the primary responsibility for elucidating, assessing, and solving these problems; courts will have to consider whether the action of school authorities constitutes good faith implementation of the governing constitutional principles. Because of their proximity to local conditions and the possible need for further hearings, the (federal) courts which originally heard these cases can best perform this judicial appraisal. Accordingly, we believe it appropriate to remand the cases to those courts. But it should go without saying that the vitality of these constitutional principles (enunciated in *Brown*) cannot be allowed to yield simply because of disagreement with them.

The courts will require that school districts make a prompt and reasonable start to integrate the schools. Once such a start has been made, the courts may find that additional time is necessary to carry out the ruling in an effective manner. The burden rests upon the defendants to establish that such time is necessary in the public interest and is consistent with good faith compliance with the decision at the earliest practicable date. To that end, the courts may consider problems related to administration, arising from the physical condition of the school plant, the school transportation system, personnel, revision of school districts and attendance areas into compact units to achieve a system of determining admission to the public schools on a nonracial basis, and revision of local laws and regulations which may be necessary in solving the foregoing problems. They will also consider the adequacy of any plans the defendants may propose to meet these problems and to effectuate a transition to a racially nondiscriminatory school system. During this period of transition, the courts will retain jurisdiction of these cases.

Relief Sought: Further argument on the question of relief from *Brown v. Board of Education,* 347 U.S. 483 (Kans. 1954)

Issue: How shall the transition to a system of public education freed of racial discrimination be made?

Significance

Any cases arising under the *Brown* decision of May 17, 1954 will be under the jurisdiction of the federal district court in the state in which the cases arise, and will not be entertained in the state court system. It is so ordered.

CASE CITATION: *Brown v. Board of Education (Enforcement Decree), 349 U.S. 294 (1955)*

87 **Desegregation**

The Governor and Legislature of the State of Arkansas defied the court order and continued to bar children on racial grounds from attending schools where the races would be mixed. Specifically at issue was the Little Rock School Board's plan to do away with segregated public schools in that city. The Little Rock Board sought to halt the enforcement of the plan for 2½ years pending further challenge and testing in the courts. The United States Supreme Court rejected the contentions.

Relief Sought: Determination whether there is no duty on state officials to obey federal court orders resting on the Supreme Court's interpretation of the United States Constitution

Issue: Are the Governor and Legislature of a state bound to obey court orders such as that in *Brown v. Board of Education?*

Holding of the District Court: For the school board

Holding of the Court of Appeals: Reversed

Holding of the United States Supreme Court: Affirmed

Reasoning

While the school board in Little Rock was going ahead in good faith with our order in *Brown,* other state authorities, in contrast, were actively pursuing a program designed to perpetuate in Arkansas the system of racial segregation which this Court had held violated the Fourteenth Amendment. The state Constitution was amended commanding the legislature to oppose "in every Constitutional manner the Un-constitutional desegregation decisions of May 17, 1954 and May 31, 1955 of the United States Supreme Court." Other laws were likewise passed to avoid our decision. The Governor used "drastic opposing action" by dispatching units of the Arkansas National Guard to Central High School, and placed the school "off limits" to colored students. Thereupon the Board asked for this delay. In the interests of the students who will be deprived of their constitutional rights thereby, we cannot grant it. The principles announced in the *Brown* decision and the obedience of the states to them, according to the command of the Constitution, are indispensable for the protection of the freedoms guaranteed by our fundamental charter for all of us. Our constitutional ideal of equal justice under law is thus made a living truth.

Significance

A court order is backed by the government, and all branches of the government must take heed of it, including the executive, legislative and judicial departments of the state. One does not have to be party to a decision to be bound thereby. The Constitution is still the "supreme law of the land, anything in the Constitution or Laws of any State to the Contrary notwithstanding."

CASE CITATION: *Cooper v. Aaron, 358 U.S. 1 (Ark. 1958)*

88 The Track System of Education

Negro children constitute more than 90 percent of the school population in the District of Columbia school system. The median annual per pupil expenditure ($292) in the predominantly (85–100%) Negro elementary schools has been $100 below the median annual per pupil expenditure for its predominantly (85–100%) white schools ($392). Generally, the white schools were underpopulated while the Negro schools were generally overcrowded. All white schools had kindergartens; some Negro schools were without them. Buildings were likewise not comparable. The track system, a form of grouping, tended to divide and separate Negroes into the "Basic" track and very few of them were in the "Honors" track. Claim was made that such an arrangement deprived Negro ghetto children of their right to equal educational opportunity.

Relief Sought: Elimination of certain educational practices from the District of Columbia public schools

> *Issue:* Does the "tracking system" deprive certain ghetto children of their right to equal educational opportunity?
>
> *Holding of the District Court:* For plaintiffs
>
> *Holding of the Circuit Court of Appeals:* Affirmed

Reasoning

In sum, all of the evidence in this case tends to show that the Washington school system is a monument to the cynicism of the power structure which governs the voteless capitol of the greatest country on earth. The remedy is as follows: 1) Injunction against racial and economic discrimination; 2) abolition of the track system; 3) abolition of the optional zones; 4) transportation for volunteering children in overcrowded school districts east of Rock Creek Park to underpopulated schools west of the Park; 5) defendants to file a plan with the court to eliminate racial and economic discrimination by October 2, 1967; and 6) substantial integration of the faculty by October 2, 1967. . . . The aptitude tests used to assign children to the various tracks are standardized primarily on white middle class children. Since these tests do not relate to the Negro and disadvantaged child, track assignment based on such tests relegates Negro and disadvantaged children to the lower tracks from which, because of the reduced curricula and the absence of adequate remedial and compensatory education, as well as inappropriate testing, the chance of escape is remote. Education in the lower tracks is geared to what Dr. Hansen, the creator of the track system, calls the "blue collar" student. Thus such children, so stigmatized by inappropriate aptitude testing procedures, are denied equal opportunity to obtain the white collar education available to the white and more affluent children.

Significance

Separate but equal facilities are inherently unequal (from *Brown*). A system of schooling which has built-in inequities is not defensible by the board of education, and they are under a positive duty to adjust these differences be they racial, educational or economic, so that equal educational opportunity for all children is guaranteed.

CASE CITATION: *Hobson v. Hansen, 269 F.Supp. 401 (Dist. of C. 1968)*

89 *Desegregation of Public Schools*

The United States Court of Appeals, Fifth Circuit had before it the question below: Where a school is technically desegregated but maintains a dual system of classes within the school, does the board meet the requirements under *Brown*? The Court of Appeals found that the board was in violation of a Supreme Court directive in *Alexander v. Holmes County, 396 U.S. 19*, that said in part: "that . . . school district here involved may no longer operate a dual school system based on race or color, and direct (ed) that they begin immediately to operate as unitary school systems within which no person is to be effectively excluded from any school because of race or color."

Relief Sought: Order to forthwith eliminate dual system of schools for blacks and whites

Issue: Does a school which maintains a dual system of classes within a technically desegregated school meet desegregation requirements?

Holding of the United States Court of Appeals: For the plaintiffs

Reasoning

On January 27, 1970, the District Court entered a decree approving a desegregation plan submitted by the school board. The plan called for the closing of three previously all-Negro schools and a combination of "pairing" and geographic zoning to assure the integration of the remaining schools. No mention was made either in the plan or the order as to the manner in which students were to be assigned to classes within the schools. The Board technically desegregated the schools. However, the Board has maintained a dual system of classes within the schools. In grades one through seven the classes remain intact with the same teachers that taught the pupils in the first semester. Thus all-Negro classes from the closed Negro schools with Negro teachers now exist in the purportedly integrated schools. Except for a few Negro students who formerly attended white schools under freedom-of-choice, classes from these schools remain all white. We think it was manifestly clear from Supreme Court decisions that we must eliminate not only segregated schools, but also segregated classes in those schools. Our earlier mandates are hereby amended to require that the Jackson Parish School Board shall forthwith eliminate the dual system of pupil attendance by integrating all black and predominantly all white classes within the schools, except in those cases where a class is a continuation of a course only offered in an all black or all white school.

Significance

There must be elimination under *Brown* and subsequent decisions of the federal courts of not only segregated schools, but also segregated classes within schools. A school technically integrated but having segregated classes within the school is in violation of the spirit of *Brown* and an order will issue to require the board to complete its job by also integrating classes within the supposedly desegregated school.

CASE CITATION: *Johnson v. Jackson Parish School Board, 423 F.2d 1055 (La. 1970)*

90   Separation of Church and State

In 1956 in the Village of Ossining a committee was formed known as the Creche Committee. Its membership consisted of Catholics, Protestants, and Jews. Its purpose was to solicit funds to enable the Committee to erect a Nativity Scene within the Village during the Christmas season. An application was made to the Board of Education to erect it on the school's property; the board by resolution granted the request and the scene was erected a few days before school closed for the Christmas holidays. It was dismantled before school re-convened. That year, 1956, no suit was brought, but in 1957 suit was brought to enjoin erection of the Nativity Scene on public property. The court dismissed the suit.

> *Relief Sought:* Action to enjoin erection of Nativity Scene on school lawn and for declaratory judgment

Issue: Is a school district which permits the erection of a Nativity Scene on its public property in violation of the doctrine of separation of church and state?

Holding of the Trial Court: Certiorari

Holding of the Appellate Court: For defendant school board

Reasoning

The Creche is undoubtedly a religious symbol. In viewing it, however, we are all free to interpret its meaning according to our own religious beliefs. If any public body were to limit that freedom or any public institution were to give instruction as to its meaning, there would, unquestionably, be a constitutional violation. That, however, is not the case. Here the school board has done no more than to make a small portion of its property available for the display. To that extent they have accommodated a religious, though non-denominational, group. However, the accommodation of religious groups is not *per se* unconstitutional. . . . Privileges and benefits should not be denied to individuals or organizations merely because of their religious affiliation or because they may be engaged in some activities of a religious nature. . . . Complaint dismissed with costs.

Significance

Erection of a Nativity Scene on public school property is not barred under the doctrine of separation of church and state. Where it was not up during school hours, no money was spent by the state to support it, and it had long been the custom for the school officials to permit erection of symbols on school property, there was no violation of the doctrine of the separation of church and state.

CASE CITATION: *Baer v. Kolmorgen, 181 N.Y.S.2d 230 (N.Y. 1958)*

AUTHOR'S COMMENTARY

Absolute separation is not and never has been required by the Constitution. Mr. Justice Douglas, speaking for the majority of the United States Supreme Court in *Zorach v. Clauson,* 343 U.S. at page 312 said:

The First Amendment, however, does not say that in every and all respects there shall be separation of Church and State. Rather, it studiously defines the manner, the specific way, in which there shall be no concert or union or dependency one on the other. That is the common sense of the matter. Otherwise, the state and religion would be aliens to each other—hostile, suspicious, and even unfriendly.

In the *Baer* case, *supra* injunctive relief was denied for lack of evidence of "irreparable injury" to plaintiffs. A basic requirement for a decree of permanent injunction is danger of irreparable injury. One plaintiff was a taxpayer, but the court said he had no "interest" in the case of such a peculiar, special or personal nature as to entitle him to relief. Nor did the municipal law granting the right of action to a taxpayer to prevent illegal acts apply to the board of education. While parents who were plantiffs did have some "interest," the possibility that their grade school children would ever attend the junior-senior high school where the Nativity Scene was located was doubtful, and entirely speculative. Nor could a parent who had a child in the junior-senior high school be heard to complain, since his child did not attend the school during Christmas vacation when the scene was on display. Even if he did, the parent would have to show irreparable injury for the permanent injunction to lie. This of course he could not do.

The accommodation of religious groups by the school board is not required by the constitution, but absolute separation of church and state is also not required. Somewhere in between lies the operational area where accommodation can and should take place.

91   *Baccalaureate Exercises*

Plaintiffs as taxpayers brought this action to enjoin claimed practices: 1) holding of baccalaureate exercises in the Baptist church; 2) holding commencement in the Presbyterian church; and 3) dissemination of religious pamphlets through the public schools. There was no dispute over the facts. Churches were the only buildings in the Lindrith community with sufficient seating capacity to accommodate the crowd which attended these services. The district court rendered judgment in favor of defendants (teacher and principal) and plaintiffs appealed. The New Mexico Supreme Court affirmed in part and reversed in part the trial court below.

Relief Sought: Injunction to bar dissemination of religious materials in public schools, and to permanently bar defendants from teaching in the public schools of the state.

Issue: Does distribution of religious literature and holding of baccalaureate exercises in a church permanently bar teachers from teaching under New Mexico law?

Holding of the Trial Court: For defendant teacher and principal

Holding of the Appellate Court: Reversed on literature question; affirmed on right to hold baccalaureate and commencement in churches

Reasoning

In *Zellers v. Huff*, 236 P.2d 949 we earlier asserted the state's commitment to the doctrine of separation of Church and State. We reassert it here. However, we do not believe this doctrine requires us to prohibit the holding of these time-honored programs in a building where all who desire to attend may be accommodated. Neither are we fearful that those conducting the services or exercises will fail to observe the proprieties of the occasion and thus give offense to anyone attending. . . . Dissemination in a public school, however, of sectarian literature is another and different situation. We condemned this practice in *Zellers,* and we condemn it here, and hold the trial court was in error when it failed to enjoin such action on the part of the defendants. The pamphlets were kept in the room where Anson taught, but we assume such could only happen with the approval of the principal, Cooper. We will not, however, overturn the action of the trial court in refusing to bar the defendants from employment as teachers in the public schools of the state.

Significance

The doctrine of separation of Church and State does not bar a school from holding baccalaureate exercises in a church where churches are the only buildings large enough to accommodate the crowd at these affairs. However, the dissemination of religious literature is barred in a public school under the same doctrine.

CASE CITATION: *Miller v. Cooper, 244 P.2d 520 (N. Mex. 1952)*

92 *Teacher Dismissal*

Plaintiff was a teacher in the Orleans Parish public schools. He would not permit the principal of his school to enter his classroom for the purpose of assisting him in improving his mode and method of instruction. At a later date, he also refused to admit a school-employed consultant, and other persons for the same purpose. The Board of Education suspended the plaintiff-teacher, and a hearing was held. Plaintiff claimed that the reason he was suspended was that the board was prejudiced because of plaintiff's support of segregation in the public schools. On the basis of plaintiff's conduct, the board dismissed him for "incompetency" and "wilful neglect of duty" under the terms of the Teacher Tenure Act of Louisiana.

Relief Sought: Reinstatement to the position of teacher with back pay

Issue: Does a teacher's refusal to permit the principal and other consultants to enter the classroom constitute "incompetency" for which he may be dismissed?

Holding of the Trial Court: For the board

Holding of the Appellate Court: Affirmed

Reasoning

Incompetency is not definitely defined in the law, so one must go to the circumstances in each case to determine what it means. Quoting *Beilan v. Bd. of Educ.*, 357 U.S. 399 (Pa. 1958) : "By engaging in teaching, in the public schools, the teacher does not give up his right to freedom of belief, speech, or association. He does, however, undertake obligations of frankness, candor, and cooperation in answering inquiries made of him by his employer board of education examining into his fitness to serve it as a public school teacher." And from *Adler v. Bd. of Educ.*, 342 U.S. 485 (N.Y. 1952) : "A teacher works in a sensitive area within a schoolroom. There he shapes the attitudes of young minds towards the society in which we live. In this, the state has a vital concern. It must preserve the integrity of the schools. That the school authorities have the right and the duty to screen the officials, teachers, and employees as to their fitness to maintain the integrity of the schools as a part of ordered society, cannot be doubted."

Significance

Although incompetency is not clearly defined in the law, it means in relative terms that a teacher is "unfit, disqualified, unable to teach, lacking in some capacity to teach, or has other disabling qualities." Each fact situation must rest upon its own merits, and no one can tell in advance whether a charge of incompetency will lie in any given situation. Incompetency is for the jury to determine on proper instructions from the court.

CASE CITATION: *Tichenor v. Orleans Parish School Board, 144 So.2d 603 (La. 1962)*

93 *Teacher Dismissal*

Plaintiff was a speech teacher in junior-senior high school classes. Complaint was brought by one of the boys in his classes that he had discussed matters dealing with sex in an improper manner during the course of the class periods. An investigation by the superintendent was conducted and conferences held with the plaintiff, in which the latter made certain admissions, after which the teacher was suspended without pay. Specific written charges were drawn up, and plaintiff sought a hearing with the board. The hearing was duly held, after which the plaintiff was discharged on action of the board. The trial court held for the board and plaintiff appealed.

Relief Sought: Reinstatement to the position of teacher

Issue: Did his discussions of sex matters in a speech class constitute bad behavior warranting his discharge by the board of education?

Holding of the Trial Court: For defendant board of education

Holding of the Appellate Court: Affirmed

Reasoning

The board's conclusions of law determined that both charges against the relator, lack of good behavior and inefficiency, have been proved. However, we entertain considerable doubt whether the findings do support the charge of inefficiency when such findings are considered in connection with certain undisputed testimony in the record. Except for the occasions constituting lack of good behavior, relator taught all of the material outlined in the textbook for his class. All students were given opportunity to speak and to discourse upon the topics at hand. The record indicates that in respect to everything but his bad behavior, his work was satisfactory—in fact, commended by his superior. If the time devoted to discussion of the problems of sex had been spent instead discussing the United Nations or the atomic bomb, we doubt if discharge on the grounds of inefficiency on such conduct could be upheld. The suspension of relator without pay is invalidated and his dismissal affirmed.

Significance

A teacher who teaches sex matters in class, particularly those outside the science field, does so at his own risk. Sex education is a subject field, and should be taught only by those having special preparation to teach it. See the following Author's Commentary for further comment on this point of view.

CASE CITATION: *State ex rel. Wasilewski v. Board of School Directors of the City of Milwaukee, 111 N.W.2d 198 (Wisc. 1961)*

AUTHOR'S COMMENTARY

In a concurring opinion, Martin, Chief Justice, and Hallows, J. concurred, but added the following comments concerning the teaching of sex education in the public schools:

> Sex education is a subject matter for which a teacher should be especially competent to teach. A parent and the school authorities have a right to expect that children are not going to be exposed to comments, discussions, and personal opinions of a teacher on sex who had not been certified to teach such subject in classes which do not relate to such subjects. . . . The majority opinion fails to recognize the right of the parent to determine whether his child shall be taught about sex in the public schools. The subject is optional. The concern of the parents as to who is to teach the subject, and what his or her background and qualifications are, and the parent's right to visit the classroom in which the subject is discussed, are all ignored in the majority opinion. Only one qualified and so certified by the proper authorities should be allowed to teach this delicate subject and only in a class expressly held for that purpose. . . .
>
> Under the majority opinion, any unqualified, unauthorized person, entirely unfit, may have his fling at teaching or instructing in sex education with little fear of the consequences, except perhaps mild censure, unless the school board adopts a rule prohibiting such activity. It seems to us to be bad in itself, not bad because it is prohibited, *mala in se,* not *mala prohibita.* . . . As an intelligent person trained to teach at the high school level, relator should have realized that his conduct was improper.

94   *Revocation of Teaching Certificate*

Plaintiff engaged in a limited, non-criminal physical relationship of a homosexual nature with another male teacher. Neither sodomy nor oral copulation was involved. The other male teacher revealed the activities at a later date. Plaintiff had never been accused or convicted of any criminal activity whatever, and the record contained no evidence of any abnormal activity or desires by the plaintiff for over six years following the event. This was the only time the plaintiff ever engaged in a homosexual act with anyone. The State Board revoked plaintiff's certificate charging "moral turpitude" which in California is grounds for mandatory revocation of the certificate. Plaintiff brought this suit seeking re-issuance of his certificate.

   Relief Sought: Mandamus to compel the State Board of Education to restore the certificate to teach

  Issue: Did the State Board, in revoking plaintiff's certificate for "moral turpitude," violate his rights?

  Holding of the Trial Court: Sustained the State Board's action

  Holding of the California Supreme Court: Reversed

Reasoning

In deciding this case, we are not unmindful of the public interest in the elimination of unfit elementary and secondary school teachers. But petitioner is entitled to a careful and reasoned inquiry into his fitness to teach by the Board of Education before he is deprived of his right to pursue his profession. The power of the state to regulate professions and conditions of government employment must not arbitrarily impair the right of the individual to live his private life apart from his job, as he deems fit. We do not hold, of course, that homosexuals must be permitted to teach in the public schools of California. What is required is that the board properly find, pursuant to the precepts set forth in this opinion, that an individual is not fit to teach. The board called no medical, psychological, or psychiatric experts to testify as to whether a man who has had a single, isolated and limited homosexual contact would be likely to repeat such conduct in the future. The board offered no evidence that a man of his background was any more likely than the average adult male to engage in any untoward conduct with a student. . . . The lack of evidence is particularly significant because the board failed to show that plaintiff's conduct in any manner affected his performance as a teacher. There was not the slightest suggestion that plaintiff had ever attempted, sought or even considered any form of physical or otherwise improper relations with any student. There is no evidence that plaintiff's conduct affected students, or his co-workers. We therefore order his certificate reinstated.

Significance

Homosexual behavior although not universally condoned cannot be used as a basis for dismissal of a public school teacher unless there is some evidence that it affects his teaching effectiveness.

  CASE CITATION: *Morrison v. State Board of Education, 82 Cal.Rptr. 175 (Calif. 1969)*

AUTHOR'S COMMENTARY

The *Morrison* case reversed in part an earlier ruling by the same court, the Supreme Court of California, although the court did distinguish the earlier case from *Morrison*. In *Sarac v. State Board of Education,* 57 Cal.Rptr. 69 (Calif. 1967) the court had before it a case similar to that in *Morrison,* except that the homosexual behavior took place in a public place instead of the privacy of the home, and plaintiff was convicted in a municipal court on a charge of homosexuality, two factors missing in *Morrison*. In upholding the State Board and ruling against the teacher, the court connected the teacher's homosexual conduct in public and the board's revocation of his teaching certificate "for obvious unfitness." While not condoning the activities condemned in *Sarac,* the court in *Morrison* held that before the state board could revoke the teaching certificate, it must logically show a connection between the teacher's homosexual behavior and his competency or incompetency to teach in the public schools. What the court was saying, it seems to this writer, is that, although the courts will not uphold homosexual behavior *per se,* if one is to have his certificate—in effect his means of livelihood—taken away, he is at least entitled to a fair and impartial hearing on the merits of the case.

In California, immoral conduct ("moral turpitude") is grounds for mandatory revocation of the teaching certificate; hence, this label should not be loosely applied, since the punishment is quite serious and not to be taken lightly. It thus behooves the board to support its case in court with substantive evidence that the behavior complained of affects the teacher's performance as a teacher, thus lowering his effectiveness in the classroom. Presumption of innocence is with plaintiff until the board's evidence tips the scales.

95   Right to Hold Outside Employment

Evelyn Horosko, although known as Miss Horosko, actually was the wife of William Connors, who managed a restaurant and beer garden located across the road from the school. There she acted as waitress, and occasionally served as bartender after school hours and during summer vacations. In the presence of her pupils, she sometimes took a drink of beer, served beer to customers, shook dice with customers for drinks, and showed customers how to play the pinball machine. She acted in this capacity for about three years. She was rated by her superintendent as 43 percent "competent," a rating of 50 percent being the "passing" or average mark. Pennsylvania law permits teachers to be dismissed on the grounds of incompetency, but does not define the meaning of the term as applied to teachers. When the board dismissed Miss Horosko, she sought equity in the court.

Relief Sought: Reinstatement to the position of teacher

Issue: Does outside employment of certain kinds amount to "incompetency" for which a public school teacher may legally be dismissed?

Holding of the Trial Court: Reinstatement

Holding of the Appellate Court: Reversed

Reasoning

The term "incompetency" has a common and approved usage, giving the term a wider meaning not limited alone to the ability to teach or knowledge of the subject to be taught. Is such a course of conduct immoral or intemperate, and does it, in combination with her scholastic and efficiency rating, amount to incompetency? We hold it to be self evident that under the intent and meaning of the act (to dismiss), incompetence is not essentially confined to a deviation from sex morality; it may be such a course of conduct as offends the morals of the community and is a bad example to the youth whose ideals a teacher is supposed to foster and to elevate. Nor need incompetency be confined strictly to overindulgence in alcoholic liquors; temperance implies moderation and a person may be intemperate in conduct without being an alcoholic addict. And so as to incompetency: as we take it, this means under the act incompetence as a teacher, but does it mean that competence is merely the ability to teach the Three R's? We would not wish to limit it in this way.

Significance

Incompetency, as applied to the role of teacher, is wider than merely the capacity to teach the Three R's, and may extend to the life of the teacher outside the classroom. If her conduct is embarrassing to the board of education, and/or goes against community mores, it may form the basis for dismissal on grounds of incompetency.

CASE CITATION: *Horosko v. Mount Pleasant Township School District, 6 A.2d 866 (Pa. 1939)*

AUTHOR'S COMMENTARY

Many teachers hold outside employment other than the work they perform in the nation's classrooms. While the cases on the question of whether holding outside employment makes the teacher incompetent are few in number, it is generally held that such outside activity turns not on a constitutional, but on a contractual consideration. The *Horosko* case *supra* is an example of this type of holding, where it was determined that the *nature* of the outside job was an embarrassment to the board of education and to the community.

In Illinois, an agriculture teacher, while employed by a board of education on a full 12 months' contract, was simultaneously engaged in private business. He spent increasing amounts of time on this business, until the board had an interview with him, and requested him to give up his business interests and teach full time or limit his business activities and give more time to his teaching duties. He refused to give the board a definite answer, saying his future actions depended in part upon the success of his business interests. The board thereupon dismissed him and he sought reinstatement. *Meredith v. Board of Education of Community Unit School District No. 7,* 130 N.E.2d 5 (Ill. 1955).

The court upheld the dismissal. "It is the job of the board to determine whether the teacher's outside activities had progressed to such an extent as to interfere with the performance of his duties as a member of the teaching staff. The best interests of the schools of the district is the guiding star of the Board of Education and for the courts to interfere with the execution of the powers of the board in that respect is an unwarranted assumption of authority, and can only be justified in cases where the board has acted maliciously, capriciously, and arbitrarily."

It appears from these and similar cases that not only the nature of the outside activities but also the extent to which it limits teacher effectiveness are for the consideration of the board in dismissal cases.

96   *Workmen's Compensation*

The superintendent of schools in this small Colorado school district arrived at school about 8:00 A.M. one morning to find that the roof of the school building was leaking from melting snow. Buckets were placed on the hallway floor to catch dripping water. The superintendent then climbed a ladder to the roof of the school gymnasium, about fifteen feet above the ground, for the obvious purpose of inspecting the extent of the damage and to determine what could be done to alleviate the situation. About 8:20 A.M. the superintendent was observed on the roof, sans overcoat, shoveling snow from the roof. He was also seen some thirty minutes later in the school library. He had concluded his shoveling activity and come down from the roof. At this point, the witness said the superintendent did not seem to be himself, that his face was red and after a brief conversation, he "rushed out." Shortly thereafter, while making preparations to go back on the roof, he collapsed and died. Cause of death was "myocardial infarction," and the examining physician said there probably "was a causal relationship between the exertion that occurred on the roof and the man's ultimate demise." On the other hand, a doctor called by the plaintiffs testified that there was no relationship nor connection. The Industrial Commission held for the widow in stating that the claim should be paid.

> *Relief Sought:* Recovery of death benefits under workmen's compensation

Issue: Did employee superintendent's death result from a job-connected injury?

Holding of the Colorado Supreme Court: Affirmed

Reasoning

Shoveling snow is not one of the normal duties of the superintendent, he being the superintendent of the school system and not its janitor. He was doing something more than just his own duties, which amounts to overexertion. The employer and its carrier claim there is no proof of overexertion, and the details are missing. We are of the view that the employer and its carrier are arguing for detail and a degree of proof not required by the workmen's compensation act. The degree of proof required of any claimant in a workmen's compensation proceeding is neither one of mathematical certainty nor one of proof beyond a reasonable doubt. Rather, in order to prevail the claimant must prove his right to compensation benefits by a preponderance of the evidence. This we believe he has done.

Significance

Where the facts show that there was an accident or overexertion which arise out of the decedent's employment, and which constituted the proximate cause of the death of the employee, the courts will tend to uphold benefit claims by the widow and family of the deceased employee.

CASE CITATION: *Baca County School District No. RE-6 v. Brown, 400 P.2d 663 (Colo. 1965)*

97 *Loyalty Oaths for Teachers*

The Arizona loyalty oath for teachers read: "I,   (name)   , do solemnly swear (or affirm) that I will support the Constitution of the United States and the Constitution and laws of the State of Arizona; that I will bear true faith and allegiance to the same, and defend them against all enemies, foreign and domestic, and that I will faithfully and impartially discharge the duties of the office of (Name of office) according to the best of my ability, so help me God (or so I do affirm) ." The legislature further stipulated that anyone who took the oath and who "knowingly and wilfully becomes or remains a member of the communist party" or any other subversive group shall be subject to prosecution for perjury and for discharge from public office. Plaintiff refused to take the oath and challenged its constitutionality. In a 5–4 decision, the United States Supreme Court declared the oath unconstitutional.

Relief Sought: Determination of the constitutionality of the Arizona loyalty oath for teachers

Issue: Was the Arizona loyalty oath for teachers unnecessarily broad and vague, hence unconstitutional?

Holding of the United States Supreme Court: Declared the oath unconstitutional

Reasoning

In previous cases involving oaths, "membership clauses" were upheld on the grounds they applied only to active membership with the specific intent of assisting in achieving the unlawful ends of the organization. There is no room for one who "does not subscribe to the organization's unlawful means" but who nevertheless is a member. Would it be legal to join a seminar group predominantly communist and therefore subject to control by those who are said to believe in the overthrow of the government by force and violence? Juries might convict though the teacher did not subscribe to the wrongful aims of the organization. And there is apparently no machinery provided for getting clearance in advance. . . . Those who join an organization but do not share its unlawful purposes and who do not participate in its unlawful activities surely pose no threat, either as citizens or as public employees. Laws such as this which are not restricted in scope to those who join with the "specific intent" to further illegal action impose, in effect, a conclusive presumption that the member shares the unlawful aims of the organization. . . . It rests on the doctrine of "guilt by association" which has no place here. The act threatens the cherished freedom of association protected by the First Amendment, made applicable to the States through the Fourteenth Amendment.

Significance

This case adds to the other criteria, this new criterion to be met by loyalty legislation: no penalties could accrue unless the individual member of an organization could be shown to have joined with the specific intent to further the unlawful purposes of the organization or to have participated in them.

CASE CITATION: *Elfbrandt v. Russell, 86 S.Ct. 1238 (Ariz. 1966)*

AUTHOR'S COMMENTARY

Loyalty oaths for teachers came into vogue following World War I, and proliferated during the McCarthy era following World War II. State legislatures were challenged during the sixties, however, and several states had loyalty oaths struck down. See *Wieman v. Updegraff,* 344 U.S. 182 (Okla. 1952); *Baggett v. Bullit,* 84 S.Ct. 1316 (Wash. 1964); *Elfbrandt v. Russell,* 86 S.Ct. 1238 (Ariz. 1966); *Brush v. St. Bd. of Higher Educ.,* 422 P.2d 268 (Ore. 1966); *Keyishian v. Bd. of Regents,* 87 S.Ct. 675 (N.Y. 1967); and *Vogel v. County of Los Angeles,* 64 Cal.Reptr. 409 (Calif. 1967). Most of these were struck down for "vagueness."

The United States Supreme Court struck down as unconstitutional an Arkansas statute which compelled every teacher, as a condition of employment in a state-supported school or college, to file annually an affidavit listing without limitation every organization to which he belonged or regularly contributed within the preceding five years. *Shelton v. Tucker,* 364 U.S. 479 (Ark. 1960).

There then followed a wave of new loyalty oaths, quite innocuous in wording and reach, which were declared constitutional. *Knight v. Board of Regents,* 390 U.S. 36 (N.Y. 1967); *Ohlson v. Phillips,* 304 F.Supp. 1152 (Colo. 1970). In *Knight,* the new oath which was upheld by the Supreme Court of the United States contains these words: "I do solemnly swear (or affirm) that I will support the constitution of the United States of America and the constitution of the State of New York, and that I will faithfully discharge, according to the best of my ability, the duties of the position of _____ to which I am now assigned." The Colorado revised oath is similarly worded.

98   *Due Process in Dismissal of a Teacher*

The principal of the high school where plaintiff taught notified the superintendent that plaintiff had been guilty of improper conduct with certain girls in his class, whereupon the superintendent recommended to the board that plaintiff be suspended pending investigation of the charges. Michigan law requires that cancellation of a teacher's contract be preceded by a hearing, at which testimony under oath was required. Plaintiff requested a public hearing on the merits, and indicated that some 100 of his friends would be present. The board, however, chose to hold the meeting in a room which had only 24 seats in addition to those at the table occupied by the board. There were no seats available for the plaintiff's friends and witnesses and it was impossible for any of them to gain entrance to the room. A request was made to the board to adjourn the meeting to a larger room nearby; the request was refused. Following the hearing, plaintiff was discharged.

Relief Sought: Reinstatement to the position of teacher

Issue: Did the hearing afforded the plaintiff meet the requirements of "due process"?

Holding of the Trial Court: For board

Holding of the Michigan Supreme Court: Reversed

Reasoning

It should be noted that the issue of whether plaintiff had a fair hearing before the school board does not in any way control the issue of whether or not he should have been discharged as a teacher. The issue is whether or not under the circumstances he had a fair and impartial hearing on the merits. As a matter of fact, plaintiff did not have a fair and impartial hearing. There is in the record before us substantial and competent evidence to support the finding that he was denied his "day in court" and we hereby order that he be reinstated to his position as teacher immediately. The board may not "go through the motions" in conducting a hearing. It must be fully aware of the rights of the plaintiff teacher and "go out of its way" to see that he is accorded his rights to a fair and impartial hearing.

Significance

The question of a fair and impartial hearing will not be raised unless there is evidence to support the idea that the board acted hastily, or in an arbitrary or capricious manner. The central question is: "Is it fair?" It must not be merely a gesture without any genuine effort to ascertain the facts of the case and to judge the outcome on the merits. The board, in its quasi-judicial capacity, in holding a hearing, must handle its responsibility with great care to avoid having its decisions set aside by the courts.

CASE CITATION: *Rehberg v. Board of Education of Melvindale, 77 N.W.2d 131 (Mich. 1956)*

AUTHOR'S COMMENTARY

The board of education has legislative, executive and quasi-judicial powers. When exercising its right to sit in judgment, it must afford the employee every courtesy to see that a fair and impartial hearing is provided. Anything short of this high standard will be questioned by the courts, and the board's decision struck down.

In Connecticut, a teacher was accorded a hearing before the board. He alleged the hearing accorded him did not meet the legal requirements in that he was not given a copy of the charges against him, had not been permitted to cross-examine witnesses, and that the decision to dismiss him on the grounds of gross inefficiency had not been proven. *Conley v. Board of Education of City of New Britain,* 123 A.2d 747 (Conn. 1956). The trial lasted for five days, the teacher had been permitted to examine the board's minutes, records, and files, and the hearing had been postponed in order to enable him to prepare his case. He had summoned witnesses, and his witnesses had been publicly advised that they would not be punished for testifying in his behalf. The court was unwilling to overthrow the finding of the board under these conditions, and held that the teacher had indeed had a full and fair opportunity to present his side of the controversy.

Some states permit *de novo* trials in the courts following a hearing by the board, which in effect gives the courts original rather than appellate jurisdiction in such cases. Other states provide for the giving of new evidence in court in addition to the review of the record of the board's hearing. The point to remember is that board findings are subject to appeal; the board, therefore, should weigh the evidence carefully else its decision be overthrown on appeal. The services of a capable school board attorney are essential, since the board members are not expected to know how to conduct a legal hearing on their own.

99   *In-Service Requirement*

Alvina Last in 1934 completed two years of college. Between 1934 and 1960 she had not pursued any further formal education. In 1958 her school board made a differential in the salary schedule dependent upon further college training for those who had less than four years of college. Mrs. Last ignored the board's rule. Her contract in 1960–61 said in part: "Said teacher must earn 6 additional semester hours of acceptable college credit by March 13, 1961, or contract will not be renewed for 1961–62." In June, 1960 she enrolled in two correspondence courses, but by the time of her dismissal in March, 1961 neither had been completed. The board assigned the following reasons for her dismissal: 1) disregard of warnings given in 1958, 1959 and 1960; 2) failure to heed the 6 semester hour warning; and 3) failure to comply with the 1960–61 contract.

Relief Sought: Reinstatement to former position as teacher

Issue: May a school board require a tenured teacher to comply with a board rule requiring in-service college courses for renewal of contract?

Holding of the Trial Court: For plaintiff

Holding of the Appellate Court: Reversed

Reasoning

A school board rule requiring all teachers without degrees to earn six semester hours of college credit is reasonable. Professional growth on the job is a proper basis for continuing a teacher in employment. There is a statute which provides that "boards may require teachers to furnish evidence of physical fitness and continued professional growth," but irrespective of legislative fiat, we conclude that boards have this power without the law so long as the requirement is reasonable. Boards of education are the proper tribunals to determine whether a teacher should be dismissed for cause and upon administrative review their findings and conclusions are considered *prima facie* true and correct. To expect the board to wait beyond the normal time for hiring teachers to determine if Mrs. Last would complete and pass her courses before hiring another teacher is most unreasonable in itself. "The best interest of the schools of the district is the guiding star of the board of education and for the courts to interfere with the exercise of powers of the board is unwarranted assumption of authority," *Meredith v. Bd. of Educ.,* 130 N.E.2d 5 (Ill. 1955).

Significance

Even in the absence of a statute permitting it, the board has the power to require professional growth of the tenured teacher, so long as the requirement is reasonable in the light of the best interest of the schools.

CASE CITATION: *Last v. Board of Education, 185 N.E.2d 282 (Ill. 1962)*

100 Guidance and Counseling Services

The parents of a deceased girl brought suit against the director of guidance and counseling in a state college to recover damages for wrongful death of their daughter, who had committed suicide about six weeks after the counselor, who had worked with her and given her various tests, had suggested that the interview series be terminated. Plaintiffs alleged negligence in the performance of the counseling duties on the part of defendant, because he had failed to provide proper guidance to the girl, had concluded the conferences, and had failed to advise plaintiffs as parents of the true condition of their daughter's mental state and condition.

Relief Sought: Recovery for damages for wrongful death of daughter

Issue: Did defendant exercise sufficient care in counseling plaintiff's daughter who committed suicide?

Holding of the Trial Court: For defendant

Holding of the Appellate Court: Affirmed

Reasoning

We are concerned here with the standard of care which a person with the training and experience of defendant might be expected to exercise in dealing with the decedent. Defendant is not trained as a medical doctor, nor is he a psychiatrist. The jury would have to speculate in order to arrive at the conclusion that defendant knew, or should have known the state of mind of the decedent, and have taken measures to avoid her suicide. To require a teacher or counselor to recognize and diagnose a medical problem would require a duty beyond reason. Therefore, the complaint by plaintiffs that the counselor should have known and recognized the decedent's condition and the state of her mind was insufficient to state a cause of action.

Significance

The courts will take into consideration the experience and training of a defendant guidance counselor in determining whether he provided the standard of care to which decedent was entitled in a suit for damages against him. The defendant can be held to only that standard of care which the ordinary adult of the same training and experience would display under the same or similar circumstances.

CASE CITATION: *Bogust v. Iverson, 102 N.W.2d 228 (Wisc. 1960)*

AUTHOR'S COMMENTARY

Although guidance counselors are to be found in nearly every school, legal cases involving their work are not numerous. Cases 100 and 101 are among the few cases of record. Case No. 100 involves the standard of care to be expected from a college guidance counselor, while Case No. 101 involves the constitutional question of whether a school pupil is entitled to take his legal counsel into a guidance conference with him.

Van Allen v. McCleary, 211 N.Y.S.2d 501 (N.Y. 1961), Case No. 80 *supra* deals with the availability of student school records to persons in interest, such as the parents. The court held that parents may not be denied access to that part of their child's record which is permanent, objective and general in nature. In California, the court granted damages to students about whom information had been illegally released in violation of a statute controlling and limiting the release of information on students in the public schools. *Elder v. Anderson,* 23 Cal.Rptr. 48 (Calif. 1962).

In *Cosme v. Board of Education of the City of New York,* 270 N.Y.S.2d 231 (N.Y. 1966) the court held as in *Madera infra* that a parent does not have the right to have counsel present at a conference of school officials scheduled to discuss the temporary suspension of the child because of misconduct. In *Mallard v. Warren,* 152 S.E.2d 380 (Ga. 1966) the question before the court was whether a citizen taxpayer and a property owner had the right to a hearing in a controversy with respect to pupil assignment by the county board of education. The citizens were successful in getting a hearing.

101   *Guidance and Counseling Services*

Plaintiff's son, a tenth grade pupil, was suspended from school for behavioral difficulties without a hearing. Several months later, the school officials held a guidance conference to consider the boy's case. Plaintiff sought to have their son represented by an attorney at the conference, but were advised that this was not permissible, whereupon they sought court action to determine their rights. The U. S. District Court below enjoined the board, but the Court of Appeals reversed the judgment and vacated the injunction of the lower court.

Relief Sought: Right to have attorney present at a guidance conference

Issue: Does barring an attorney from a Superintendent's Guidance Conference violate a guaranteed right of the pupil to due process?

Holding of the Trial Court: For plaintiffs

Holding of the Appellate Court: Reversed

Reasoning

The guidance conference is not a judicial or quasi-judicial hearing. Neither the child nor his parents are being accused. In saying that the provision against the presence of an attorney for the pupil in a District Superintendent's Guidance Conference results in depriving plaintiffs of their constitutionally protected right to a hearing, the trial court misconceives the function of the conference and the role which the participants therein play with respect to the educational welfare of the child. Law and order in the classroom should be the responsibility of our respective educational systems. The court should not usurp this function and turn disciplinary problems involving suspension into criminal adversary proceedings—which they definitely are not. The rules, regulations, procedures, and practices disclosed on this record evince a high regard for the best interest and welfare of the child. The courts do well to recognize this. No one denies that to an incalculable degree the future of this Country depends inescapably upon the continued, constantly improved education of *all* its inhabitants. Nor can it very successfully be denied that the best practicable hope of attaining this objective is to be found and maintained in the public schools. But the mere attendance at the conference of counsel would do little to aid this problem without also granting the other rights accorded in adversary proceedings—calling of witnesses, cross-examinations, etc. To do so would be destructive of the original purpose of the guidance conference—to provide for the future education of the child.

Significance

Guidance conferences for the purpose of deciding what to do with a child in school are not judicial or quasi-judicial hearings, hence the board is within its rights in barring counsel from such proceedings.

CASE CITATION: *Madera v. Board of Education of the City of New York, 386 F.2d 778 (N.Y. 1968)*

AUTHOR'S COMMENTARY

The "guidance conference" referred to in Case 101 *supra* involved a number of persons concerned with various aspects of a child's behavior—social workers, psychologists, psychiatrists, as well as educators. As a result of such a conference, a suspended child may be reinstated in the same school, transferred to another school, transferred to a special school for socially maladjusted children, or have his case referred to the clinical services provided by the board of education. He might also be referred to the bureau of attendance for possible court action. It was this latter possibility which caused plaintiffs to desire to have counsel present, since one of the charges was that there had been an attack on a teacher, although plaintiff's son was only one of three boys involved in the incident.

Aside from changing the school of attendance, or referring it to the courts for possible action, the case was designed for helping the student to adjust. The court rejected the argument that the student would be deprived of his "liberty," hence the presence of counsel was not necessary as a due process requisite at the conference stage. The court avoided the question of whether being a child of urban poor and disadvantaged parents made a legal difference with respect to the child's right to have an attorney present to plead his case.

Index